A FEATHER
FOR MY LOVE

A FEATHER FOR MY LOVE

The Healing Power of After-Death Communication

Daeryl Holzer

SoulShift
Publications

FIRST EDITION

First Printing, 2023

Cover graphics by Daeryl Holzer

ISBN: 979-8-218-30415-7

SoulShift Publications

This book is dedicated to Steve Holzer,
my soulmate, who showed me how to love and be
loved, who continues to be a guiding and loving
presence, even after his death.

Contents

Introduction

We never said, "Til death do us part."
We vowed, "I will love you forever."

This is my personal story of finding my soul mate, Steve, and being enriched by our love, then struggling to save him from dying, and grappling with the misery and finality of loss. I tell of navigating through the various manifestations of grief and how I was assisted in my healing process by an ongoing stream of after-death communication from his soul.

From the very first mysterious phone message, and throughout the next nine (and possibly more) years, I have been reassured that his death was not the end, that I was still being loved and cared for. As I moved through the steps necessary to restart my life, I received help in a multitude of ways, which I can only attribute to a force beyond my own doing.

With guidance from some place beyond, I was able to let go of what was no more, while holding on to the love. Through this remarkable journey, I received meaningful insights about life and the other side and was shown techniques which brought unexpected healing for my broken heart.

My intuitive abilities and my belief in energies beyond the physical world, as well as Steve's promise, all added to our ability to stay connected. However, I truly believe that maintaining an ongoing bond with a loved one after their death is a universal possibility. Through the sharing of my story, I hope to present such an opportunity to you.

With love and grace,
Daeryl Holzer

Chapter 1

We Met in A Parking Lot

I had just arrived in Santa Fe with the focus of teaching a workshop and meeting with clients. The initial plan was for my friend to pick me up at the airport. At the last minute, she was offered a catering job at an art opening the same evening as my arrival and would no longer be able to give me a ride. Instead, she encouraged me to rent a car and join her at the opening, suggesting, "There could be important people for you to meet."

Having my plans derailed was not new to me. In fact, sudden disruptions and adjustments were more the norm in my life. I had learned that going with the flow of these unexpected changes often resulted in new opportunities, so I altered my travel plans with an attitude of hope and curiosity.

On the plane, I had time to envision the possibilities of this ten-day trip. Away from my usual responsibilities as the single mom of a teenager, who would be spending this time with a friend's family, I was now free to turn my full attention to my professional life.

For my first weekend in Santa Fe, I had scheduled a *SoulShift Healing* Workshop, a course I had developed to help people address their personal issues from the soul perspective. There were also a few days during the week set aside for private Clairvoyant Sessions. Many of my regular phone clients, as well as friends of my event host, had already registered, but I welcomed the potential for additional sign-ups whom I might meet at the art opening.

Part way through the airplane journey, my mind shifted from work to a previously not considered possibility – that I might also have some fun. Since promising my daughter that it would just be the two of us until she graduated high school and left for college, I had set aside the notion of any kind of romantic relationship. This was a healthy development for both of us. I had a history of falling in with men who were overly demanding of my time, to her detriment as well as mine. Fully intending to keep my commitment of not getting into anything that would come home with me, I mused, "I just want someone to play with!"

So here I was, parked in a dirt lot outside of a large residential compound, standing at the open trunk of my rental car, dressed up at bit and digging for a handful of my promotional brochures. With the thought of connecting to new clients, I focused my intention and sent a silent message to my unseen Spirit helpers. "I am open to meeting important people."

Out of my left side vision, a swirl of light caught my attention, as a white car backed in next to me. I looked up to see a gorgeous man with adorably unruly silver-gray hair poking his head out of the driver's side window and unabashedly beaming at me.

"Well… Hey there!"

Who would do that?

The smiling man had backed his car into the spot beside me so that he could immediately greet me, instead of being on the far side of the car. I didn't take it as creepy, but rather amusing. I thought, "Here's a man who is spontaneous, confident, and willing to appear just a bit foolish!"

His demeanor of curiosity and delight blossomed into an impish grin as he got out of his car and walked towards me. He was slim and fit, with a bounce to his step. He wore a white linen shirt with billowing sleeves and open collar tucked into faded jeans. Everything about him expressed a bohemian nature – just my type. I was instantly attracted to his blue eyes which sparkled with joyful mischievousness.

As we stood together, I felt a natural desire to wrap my arm around his waist, but of course I didn't. Walking together towards the event, I had the comfortable feeling that we had known each other forever. I learned that his name was Steve and that tonight's artist was a friend of his. He learned that I was visiting from Oregon to see clients and teach a workshop. I would have been happy to stay by his side the whole night, but the teenaged son of my friend approached us, and I was drawn away to find Judy.

"See you inside," I waved hopefully to Steve.

He flashed another radiant smile, his eyes twinkling. "See ya 'round all night!"

As is typical in Santa Fe, this expansive Spanish style home was arranged with multiple adjoining rooms forming a square around a common open-air atrium. Judy was in the center, busy tending to guests as they filled their plates from the buffet. After a brief greeting, I left her to begin mingling.

I was comfortable with the idea of engaging with the guests, and eager to meet people who might be interested in my workshop or sessions while I was in Santa Fe. The artist's paintings were displayed throughout the rooms and as I moved through the home conversing with various groups, I had more than half an eye scanning for the handsome man with the charming smile.

Where had he gone? After several hours, and several circuits through the rooms, it was time to go.

With a silly smile, I told Judy, "I'm not leaving until that man has my phone number!"

She laughed at my determination and agreed, "Okay. Go find him. Fifteen minutes!"

A few more quick loops around the now empty rooms. No Steve.

I finally found him after I extended my search beyond the main building. He was standing outside one of the small cottages on the grounds, laughing with his friends. I couldn't miss him there.

Was it the glow of his white shirt, or his soul, shining under the spotlight of the porch light?

Drawn to his radiance, I walked over without hesitation or self-consciousness. When I approached, he immediately greeted me, "Hey there! I'm glad you found me. I've been walking around in circles looking for you!"

I confessed that I too had been making my rounds through the main building in hopes of catching up with him. We shared a laugh and acknowledgment that the Universe was toying with us. He was amused by our mutual desire to find each other, and asked if he could call me. I handed him one of my workshop brochures, letting him know I'd like to see him again.

Returning to my friends, my whole being was energized by the exchange with Steve, yet my mind said, "Be satisfied with the moment and let go of expectations."

The next morning, Steve called me at Judy's home, and we talked for what must have been an hour, though neither of us were aware of time passing. We shared stories, and laughs, and learned about each other's astrological birth charts. I hung up the phone with a joyful buoyancy in my heart and excited about his invitation to dinner the following night.

I walked back into Judy's living room. She had gathered a group of friends who were interested in my professional work. Being my natural, unfiltered self, I blurted out, "Guess what? I have a date tomorrow night!"

One of the women, whom I knew as a client, was incredulous. "A DATE? Nobody dates in Santa Fe! We hook up at parties, but not real dates! What do you mean you have a date? Who is it?"

"Well, I don't know his full name, but his first name is Steve. I wrote his number on my hand."

Somewhat frantically, she reached for my arm to look at the number. Still holding on and unable to contain her shock, she blurted, "That's my old boyfriend!"

"Oh no!" I said, disappointed. My heart sank, steeling myself to the prospect that I should back out of my date with Steve. "I can call him up and cancel. I don't want to cause any weirdness." I meant what I said, maintaining my integrity of not competing with girlfriends and grateful that I hadn't gotten in too far before discovering this potential conflict.

Settling down after her initial shock and back to her more evolved self, she said, "No. Don't do that. We ended a while ago and I don't have a jealous bone in my body." (She really doesn't). "You should go."

"Okay. Well then tell me what's *wrong* with him!"

"Nothing," she said. He's intelligent, fun, and gorgeous. Just don't fall in love with him. He'll break your heart!"

Hmmm. Her warning held me back only a little. I would have run away immediately if she had described addiction, anger, or neediness, for those were the traps I had been snared in before. Since I wasn't planning on getting attached, I thought, "Why not?" Even so, her caution stuck in the back of my mind, giving me more restraint than was my norm.

The night of our dinner, Steve took me to an elegant Italian restaurant. On the way, he told me that he had looked up my website and had enjoyed my "beautiful mandala artwork." I was impressed that he had taken the initiative to check me out and I took his words as an authentic appreciation, not a contrived compliment. Over Chianti and pasta, the conversation flowed easily, more like old friends catching up after a long absence than a first date.

I was taken by his bright mind and his knowledge of the same esoteric subjects as those that interested me. He described his work as a finish carpenter, with a focus on remodeling adobe homes, which he did to fund his true passion of painting and printmaking. He had been a professional artist in one medium or another, including ceramics, his whole adult life. I was particularly impressed by the refreshing way he spoke of his personal misfortunes, with a twist of humor and acknowledgment of wisdom gained, rather than bitterness or blame.

I spoke of my delight at our unexpected encounter and the sequence of events that led me to being in that parking lot. He responded with, "Well, it seems that the Universe has conspired on our behalf!"

Then he shared with me his version of events that had led to our meeting.

"After the end of a 15-year-relationship, I found myself loose in the world. I'd had a string of escapades with the 'Sisters of Mercy,' which was fun for a time," he grinned and chuckled. "I felt bad about leaving a trail of broken hearts, so I'd sworn off going out for a while, to avoid temptation." Heavy sigh.

"And then, my artist friend, a gay woman, asked me to come to her opening. I assumed there would only be lesbians there and I wouldn't get into trouble. But of course, the very first person I saw was you, standing by your car with the sunset gleaming behind you." Beaming with an especially radiant smile, he added, "You looked so beautiful. I just couldn't help myself!"

As we shared our stories, I found his handsome face easy to get lost in. Clean-shaven tanned skin revealed a strong chin, which cradled a captivating smile. He had the rugged good looks of a movie star, the kind that drew attention, though he didn't seem even remotely aware of his charismatic appeal. His blue eyes drew me in, not in an over-powering way, but in the way sunshine glistens on water. And his laugh, his easy laugh, came to me as joy rippling through the Universe.

Leaving the restaurant, we casually held hands and crossed the parking lot towards his car. Apparently, he remembered from our phone conversation that my sun sign was Aries and expressed delight in pointing out the constellation in the clear night sky. "Right there, those three stars in a row, that's Orion's Belt. Follow it, and there's Aries! And near by, that blurry light is the Pleiades."

Gazing at the twinkling stars, we had our first kiss and for a moment, became the only two souls in the whole world. Time? Who knows. Suddenly, the sound of thunder broke, the sky shifted to clouds, and lightning flashed overhead. We laughed and ran to the car in time to avoid getting drenched as a delightful summer rain poured down around us.

After that night, I was smitten, my heart somewhere in the constellation of Aries, and my feet floating above my head! At the same time, I was realistic. We lived over 1400 miles apart, and I would keep the promise to my daughter to not rearrange our lives for a man. Setting aside any projections of the future, I allowed myself the pleasure of two more dates with Steve during my time in Santa Fe.

On the second date, he cooked a delicious salmon dinner at his home, which was set up as a large artist's studio in a converted warehouse. Some women would be put off by the lack of normal furniture and interior decorating, the cement floor, and the folding table covered in paint splatters which doubled as the dining table. I was in awe of his full-on artist's lifestyle; a large easel against the wall holding a work in progress, the shelves filled with paint pots and large paper, open notebooks strewn about showing rough sketches.

On the third date, we went to Judy's home for a dinner party. Steve was gracious and entertaining, and I enjoyed watching him interact with others. One of the guests, whom I didn't know, was intrigued by my Clairvoyant profession, so I began describing my work with clients and the concepts of the *SoulShift Workshop* I had presented the previous weekend.

A different guest reacted to the conversation by aggressively challenging my right to call myself a Clairvoyant if I hadn't been born into a lineage of mystics. As I attempted to share about my natural gifts and years of experience, the man got more and more heated in adamant defense of his own perspective. Without interfering, Steve simply took my hand, letting me know that he cared and was there if I needed him. His gesture of silent solidarity gave me the confidence and the permission I needed to call an end to that pointless conversation.

From that moment on, I knew that Steve had the ability to let me be powerful and speak up for myself and that he would respect me when I did so.

All through those first dates in Santa Fe, there was a growing fondness and a sense of being totally comfortable in each other's presence. We enjoyed each other with full abandon, focusing on the moment, without the need for words of devotion or promises. I returned home with heartfelt gratitude and guarded optimism for the future.

The rest of the summer, I focused on my life in Oregon, and Steve focused on his in Santa Fe.

As much as I intended to not get attached, I let myself enjoy getting to know him through emails and occasional phone calls. We shared more about our childhoods, our first marriages, and our similar struggles in following career passions while raising children. He too, had found himself as a single parent, raising two boys who were now grown.

As we spoke, I witnessed him dealing well with present challenges and working hard. Steve listened to me without judgment as I described some of the difficulties that I faced balancing parenting and earning a living. He didn't tell me what to do or attempt to rescue me.

Living so far apart during those first months gave us the opportunity to develop a strong basis of friendship and trust. In my past relationships, I had easily fallen in love, only to discover problems once I was in too deep. This time, I was first stepping into *like*!

Towards the end of that first summer, Steve and I formed a plan for me to visit him again in October. For this trip, I would stay at his place for ten days. In anticipation, I became a giddy bag of nerves, dancing between hope and fear. Judy encouraged me to take the chance, with her place as a back-up, so I pulled myself together and off I went.

Our time together was magical. I know everyone says that and I do think there is some magic around people who are falling in love, but there was something extraordinary about this man. (And I wasn't the only one who thought so!)

He took me out at night to his favorite spots and everywhere we went, people greeted him with joyful welcome. On a romantic motorcycle ride through the Santa Fe mountains amid the fall, yellowing Aspen trees, Steve stopped in a meadow for a surprise picnic at the exact moment I was thinking how romantic that would be. We shared home-cooked meals and long mornings chatting over coffee.

All that week, we talked and laughed, and danced, and made love. There was a notable lack of awkwardness or annoyance on both sides. Our conversations and desires were in sync, as we moved easily through our days together. In unspoken communication, our souls purred, "I *get* you!"

Chapter 2

Long Distance Soul Connection

After that trip, Steve and I made a regular habit of seeing each other. We would spend six weeks working and tending to our own lives, then ten days together without other obligations. We took turns traveling to each other's places.

He told me that he had sworn to not get involved with a woman who still had a child at home, but he said, "I'll make an exception for you. You are worth waiting for." And he did wait, for two and a half years, while my daughter was finishing high school. Each of those ten-day visits was like a honeymoon, having fun, and getting to know and love each other at deeper and deeper levels.

On one of the visits, I suggested that we explore our past lives together. This was a technique I had developed to use for myself or with clients to gain awareness of underlying dynamics. He was curious too, as we had both remarked that we felt like we had known each other forever.

Using my recording, we went on our own individual Past Life Journeys. After the guided recall, we shared what we had experienced. In Steve's journey, he was a native man walking alone in a desert, peacefully aware of living a satisfying life.

In my journey, I had been a Priestess in an ancient culture, going out into the community to offer my services of counsel and healing. My role included coordinating temple functions, as well as accepting and teaching students. I saw that Steve was also there in my temple life. His role was to observe and track the movements of the celestial bodies. At the center of the temple, open to the sky, there was a shallow pool where he would place crystals to mark the reflections of each star. In this way, noteworthy astronomical patterns could be measured and studied. I didn't gain the details of our relationship during that life, but I was clear that our paths had been entwined with mutual purpose and respect.

Steve took to heart the profound meaning of our soul connection in that previous life and created a series of silkscreen prints entitled "Stars In A Pool." I received the prototype, a single edition, entitled "Stars In A Pool For My Love." From then on, he called me, "My Love."

He wasn't the only one inspired by our blooming relationship. I was gradually embracing the possibility that I could have a solid and healthy relationship with this man who was so easy to love.

I wrote poetry to express my love and gratitude. I decorated a gold paper crown and sewed silk pajamas for his birthday to show how much I adored him. He was delighted by my playful creativity. With the inspiration and vitality that love can bring, I launched more fully into my professional Clairvoyant work and got focused on writing the book I had been patching together for six years. For us both, this was a time of affirmation and expansion.

Steve was also patiently respectful of my responsibilities with my teen-aged daughter. At first, she refused to interact with him and arranged to stay with a friend's family each time he came to visit. As a result of her experience with a boyfriend of mine, as well as her own father, she didn't want to deal with what she assumed would be "another just like the rest." And I didn't push.

When she finally did agree to meet Steve, the occasion was spurred by her friend who expressed curiosity. The two of them came together and had dinner with us. Steve was respectful and patient, with a touch of the humor that always set people at ease. Afterwards, the friend told my daughter, "Steve is cool," and so she began to open to the idea of getting to know him. The relationship between Steve and my daughter had begun.

On one visit, he spent a whole day with her in the garage, helping her to build a lightbox. He didn't build it *for* her, but instead, empowered her by teaching her the process and how to use tools. It wasn't lost on her that he didn't push her away to have me all to himself, that he was giving her the undivided attention she deserved.

Once, when I heard their laughter through the garage door, I poked my head in and asked, "What are you two laughing at?" They both chuckled conspiratorially and replied, "You!"

There was just as much talking and bonding as there was building, which was a good thing. Steve was presenting himself as a mature and considerate man, the first healthy father figure my daughter had known. Their relationship grew from then on.

Eventually, my daughter moved away to college, and I unraveled my life in Oregon to begin a full-time life with Steve. As we loaded up his truck for my move, I felt like a teenager in love, filled with excitement and hope that finally, at last, I had found my soulmate, the one I had been looking for my whole life.

We lived six months in Santa Fe while he finished up some projects, I focused on writing my book, and we prepared his 1965 Airstream to carry us to Marfa, Texas.

Marfa was a decades-long dream for him. He loved the desert, especially the nearby Big Bend National Park, and he was aligned with the kind of minimalist art that was prevalent in Marfa, as well as desiring a small-town atmosphere. I had visited there with him the year before and was more than a bit terrified of how I was going to manage a life there. Too hot, too remote, too Catholic, etc.

But. I would have gone anywhere with Steve. He was that incredible. He made me feel absolutely loved and supported. Besides, I've always been up for new adventure, and he agreed to accommodate my need to travel for work, so I held my breath and took a leap.

Chapter 3

Together At Last

We pulled into the Apache Pines Trailer Park, just outside of Marfa, mid-February 2006, in time for the launch of the new Marfa Public Radio station. Steve immediately volunteered his expert building skills to prepare the empty building for the Grand Opening, including installing an antenna on top of the roof. I did my part to organize the chaos of a newly installed phone system and assembled office furniture.

Steve and I formed an idea, "Wouldn't it be cool if there was a prop to switch on at the Grand Opening?" Putting our creative energies together, he transformed an old metal power box by adding a movable arm handle which would light up a bulb on top. I painted the box silver and decorated it with the radio station logo. The prop was a hit!

At the opening, we met many of the locals as well as notable Texan celebrities. From the start, we endeared ourselves to our new acquaintances and from then on, we were warmly welcomed in this uniquely interesting small town.

At the time we moved to Marfa, the community was the kind where the whole town would turn out for events, and everyone was included. To celebrate any number of occasions, the local families would rent out the AmVets hall, hire a Mariachi band from the nearby Mexican border town and everyone, including children and elders, would have fun dancing Cumbia and sharing the food and drink they had brought in their coolers. Steve and I both enjoyed engaging with people from all walks of life. We quickly felt at home, with a sense of being liked and included in the community.

The Apache Pines Trailer Park was old and simple, on the edge of town overlooking a wide expanse of high desert plains and ranch land. Steve had parked his Airstream here many times on his way south to visit Big Bend National Park.

Now that this was our temporary home, he told me of a momentous occurrence during a stopover a few years previous. Cruising through on his 1978 Motoguzi

Motorcycle, he had taken a mid-day break and spotted a Kestrel sitting up on one of the power poles. Steve had a special affinity with birds of prey, Kestrels in particular, and loved watching them.

The Kestrel had flown down and landed a few feet from him. Curious to see how the bird might respond, he held out his arm as an invitation, and waited. Steve wasn't inclined to make up stories – he had enough remarkable ones without needing to fabricate any – so I believed him when he described what happened next.

The Kestrel jumped up and perched on his outstretched arm! For a long moment, the bird stared quizzically at him, and then flew off, leaving Steve in awe. This communion with the Kestrel was profoundly meaningful for Steve, a 'sign' that Marfa was the right place for him.

As if to mark the rightness of our move, a few days after we arrived together at the trailer park, we witnessed a pair of Kestrels mating there, which amused us both to no end. Steve would later name his business Kestrel Design.

We lived together in the Airstream for a year, which might sound terrible to some people. Other than the ferocious winds that would rock the trailer like an ogre playing with a rattle, and not being able to entertain more than one guest at a time, our life in the Airstream was romantic, more like a long vacation. We had everything we needed in that tiny space. Instead of television, we listened to music on CDs, laughed, and read 'bedtime stories' to each other before sleep each night. These books included the unabridged *One Thousand and One Nights* and a delightful manuscript which a local friend had recently written.

Living in the Airstream, it was easy to simply hook up the truck and transport our home to Big Bend National Park for a few days. I marveled at how a brief rain could suddenly transform the brown desert into a glorious green landscape, with every cactus plant and a variety of wildflowers springing into blooms of remarkable color and beauty.

Marfa was a small town, land-locked by immense ranches and inconveniently remote for new building projects. Steve immediately found work remodeling the old adobe homes, often previously neglected or vacant, but now in high demand as the town's population was rapidly growing.

In contrast, there was very little local interest in my more esoteric career, so I began making long drives to Austin for events, continued with my phone clients, and earnestly set to complete and publish my book.

I also found a part time job doing administrative work and grant writing for a local non-profit arts foundation, which happened to have a large but underutilized ceramics studio. In college, I had been passionate about ceramics and entertained it as a career focus. Even though I ended up choosing a different path, ceramics has always remained an active hobby. Here, an opportunity to rekindle a dormant desire was presented.

Coinciding with my love of inspiring and empowering others, I set to reorganizing the studio and began teaching hand-building for adults. Eventually, I also set up a successful ceramics work program for teens which was funded through grants and donations.

Though not my main focus, I had managed to find a niche for myself in this community and in my new life with Steve.

He and I spent many spontaneous evenings out enjoying dining and live music, and dancing under the incredibly dark and star-filled night sky. Everywhere we went, we met and engaged with visitors as well as the locals of all ages who were becoming our friends. Though we were living bare bones, our lives were rich with interesting people and experiences.

Now that we were together, Steve and I were shining as bright as those desert stars, and people lit up in our presence. We consciously appreciated every moment of our new life together and recognized that we were part of a very special moment in this unique, but rapidly changing town.

Eventually, we moved into our own little adobe house, where we had more room for all our projects. With the Airstream now parked in the back yard as a guest house, we began hosting out-of-town friends as well as visitors who found us on CouchSurfing.com (a precursor to AirBnB with no money involved). In this way, even though our home was rustic and humble, we met and entertained interesting people from all over the world. I was happy that Steve enjoyed socializing as much as I did.

In 2007, we eloped.

Eloping was our way to avoid the complicated travel logistics of a remote wedding, but mostly we did it as an amusing trick to play on our local friends. We made arrangements for a wedding at the Presidio County Courthouse, a grand and beautiful nineteenth century three-story landmark. Holding the simple bouquet of flowers that Steve had gathered from people's yards that morning, and carrying the gold bands a local jeweler friend had quickly fabricated, we stood before the Judge in the cupola.

The 360-degree view of the surrounding plains was stunning, and I noted how far we could see in every direction on such a clear day. Our ceremony was short and sweet, but by the time we kissed, the sky had become filled with dark clouds and then cracked open with thunder and lightning. We took a few quick photos and scampered excitedly down several flights of stairs.

Instead of our anticipated celebratory departure, we found ourselves trapped inside by a major downpour. Steve and I stood at the front door laughing, wondering if the storm would pass any time soon. In silent agreement that we couldn't wait, we took off our shoes, held hands, and made a run for the truck. Once again, the sky was making a spectacle of our love!

Back home, we quickly emailed a wedding photo and brief notice to the local weekly paper, meeting the Tuesday deadline for the Thursday publication. Then, off we went in the Airstream for a few glorious days in Big Bend National Park. Our joy was amplified upon our return, as we were greeted by delighted friends and acquaintances.

A few months later, we threw a big community party in our backyard. There, surrounded by friends new and old, and a daughter who now called Steve "Pops," we celebrated a life full of satisfaction and potential.

I felt like all the difficult times of my life were behind me, that I was embarking on a chapter where all good things were about to unfold. We were profoundly happy together.

With the solidarity of our love and devotion to each other, we embraced our professional goals with increased passion. Rather than being distracted, we encouraged each other. New opportunities arose, as if love brought more wind to our sails. We took turns bringing in money, allowing the other person total focus on their goals.

I completed and published my book, *Opening A Window To The Soul: A Guide to Living Beyond the Human Drama*. Steve's wise input and support enabled me to do so and gave my career the boost that eventually led to my ongoing work in Japan. There, in addition to Clairvoyant sessions, I developed several comprehensive teaching programs, which I also began presenting throughout the US.

Steve created several new series of prints and paintings which were shown in local galleries. He then expanded his expression by making camera-less films, drawing and printing on old 65mm educational movies. His art vocabulary had traditionally included fractal imagery, which he manipulated in a computer program and transferred to his prints and paintings. Now, he developed techniques to transfer those patterns to a moving picture format.

In 2012, Steve's film, *Machine Deva*, won the award for *Best Experimental Art Film* at a Northwest film festival. Always amused by his own sense of humor, he described his film as, "a mind-blowing love story, or twenty minutes inside my head!"

TOGETHER AT LAST

Chapter 4

My First Brush With Death

Even though I was in my early 50s, so far, no one very close to me had died.

That all changed when my mother became ill with cancer in 2011. To help care for her, I traveled regularly to California, often sleeping on the couch in her assisting living apartment for a month at a time. After a series of painful and ineffective radiation treatments along her spine, she made the decision to stop medical intervention and embrace the end of her life.

Though I suspect she wasn't able to be as honest with others, she said calmly to me, "I've lived a good life. I'm not afraid to die."

Up until her illness, she didn't understand what I did in my professional life. As she put it, "Why do you want to get involved in other people's problems?" Now that I was in the position of caregiver, with her role being more that of a vulnerable child, she seemed to welcome my sensitivity and compassion.

I had heard other people tell of a reversal of roles when a parent neared the end of their life. For Mom and I, it felt comfortable and natural when I shifted into mothering her, and we moved easily into a closeness that we hadn't experienced before.

The last time I saw her, we looked into each other's eyes, and she asked me, "Do you know where I am going?" This type of inquiry was very out of character for her, as she had never really explored spiritual matters other than to reject organized religion. Being in awe of a beautiful sunset was her way of having a profound moment. She hadn't been interested in discussing any of the concepts I had written about in my book, other than to comment, "I wish I had known more about the connection between thinking and feeling."

Now, she was asking for my spiritual opinion, so I responded, still holding her gaze. "I know that you have always been a good person, so I am sure that you will go to a good place. And perhaps we will see each other again in a future life. I hope so."

I am grateful for those last interactions, as there seemed to be an unspoken healing between us, an authentic rapport that transcended the relationship of mother and daughter.

Back home, I settled into the notion that I had said goodbye, and tried to be at peace with the awareness that she would be passing soon and that there was little I could do for her. In my years of spiritual practice, I had learned how to shift my mind away from worry, which tends to bring a focus on 'the bad thing' happening. Instead, I would direct my attention to the energy of love and acceptance, which I did now, for Mom.

My only wish for her was that she have an easy passing and that she not suffer. As I meditated, I held the vision of a beautiful column of light, going from the ground near her, up into the infinite sky. No agenda on my part, nothing against her will, no idea of timing. I was simply sending love and an intention for her unrestricted transition, much like sweeping a path in front of one who would be walking there.

The next morning as I was waking, Mom's healthy smiling face appeared in my mind's eye. Just then, the phone rang. I sat up abruptly to answer the call from my brother telling me that mom had passed in the night.

When I returned to California a few days later, my two siblings were also there. I anticipated a time of mutual grieving and sympathy as we tended to the immediate and necessary tasks that follow death.

I wasn't prepared for the frantic disposal of Mom's household belongings and the immediate focus on counting her assets. There was no comforting each other, no kind words or reminiscing, no attempts to honor her as our mother. I was asked to write her obituary, send letters of notice to her out-of-state friends, and to collect her ashes from the mortuary, all tasks that my sister was too stressed to handle.

I understand that each person has a unique way of experiencing and expressing loss, but I wasn't prepared for the extreme display of pain that came at me next.

After spending time consoling Mom's closest lady friend, I came back to the condo, and was slammed into an argument with my siblings over a new discovery in the inheritance. Even though Mom's will defined "all to be divided equally among my three descendants," there was a sizable IRA in my adult daughter's name.

The two of them kept shouting, "This is WRONG!" and "We have to fix it!"

Their shock and anger were directed towards me, as if I would receive more money than they would, or that I had somehow influenced Mom's decisions. I tried to stay neutral and kept saying that we legally had to follow how she left things.

It wasn't the division of wealth that I defended so much as my brother's derogatory accusation that "She didn't know what she was doing!" All the while, I kept hearing Mom's voice in the back of my mind, "Stick to your guns!" So, I did. To this day, I believe she was telling me that she knew *exactly* what she was doing!

The following month, I traveled to Japan for my teaching work. On a day off, I hiked the sacred journey path to the Daibutsu (Great Buddha) in Kamakura, which had been used by monks and pilgrims for over a thousand years. My head was a muddle of conflict regarding my siblings and grief regarding my mother.

Walking among the ancient cedar trees, my troubled mind sought clarity. With each step over centuries-worn stone, my heart longed for peace. Silently, I asked Mom, "What should I do?"

Immediately, her firm reply, "Leave me out of it!" And then, nothing more.

Even though I could still feel a loving connection with Mom in the first few days after her passing, as soon as the sibling conflicts started, her responses in my mind were blunt and seemed to revert to her personality while alive, that of ignoring the life-long discord between her children.

And then, within a few weeks, nothing. I couldn't feel her presence at all anymore. There are times when I still talk to her, as if she could hear me, when I want to share something good that would please her, but she doesn't respond.

At the time, the family blowup took me by surprise, but now I realize that it is somewhat common for old childhood dynamics to surface in exaggerated ways when people are suffering after the loss of a parent. Siblings often fight over money and possessions, as they grapple to make up for an absence of love.

Steve was gracious enough to listen sympathetically to my struggle. He had witnessed enough of my sibling's behavior before Mom's death, so now, he assured me that I was justified in my perspective and shouldn't let myself be bullied. His unconditional love and support were immensely valuable, as I have often been blamed or told that it's "my responsibility to get along." Steve helped me to realize that there was no way to do so.

During the time I was taking care of mom and dealing with the aftermath of her death, I was so preoccupied with my own concerns that I missed the importance of what was going on with Steve. As was his usual way when he had any kind of problem, he didn't lean on other people and was not prone to complaining. His whole life, he had been very healthy, and only went to doctors for things like a torn shoulder injury, not regular check-ups.

Lately, he had been more tired than usual, and seemed to be losing weight. But still, I was oblivious of what was to come.

MY FIRST BRUSH WITH DEATH

Chapter 5

This Can't Be Happening!

It could have been that he knew.

It could have been that he was as shocked as I was.

When Steve finally agreed to see a doctor, he was doubled over in pain. There was no clinic in our small town, so the only option for immediate care was the Emergency Room at the Alpine Hospital, thirty miles away. After a blood draw and a full body scan, I fully anticipated some simple and treatable diagnosis. Perhaps a kidney infection or overuse of Ibuprofen.

The bad news struck me like a bomb: "He has Stage 4 Prostate Cancer which has spread throughout his body."

The intensity and unreality of the news stunned me speechless. All I could do was to lay my head down on his chest and turn my face away so that he wouldn't see my tears.

Stroking my hair, Steve's first words to me were, "I'm so sorry for how this is going to crash your life."

The ER doctor seemed in a panic, as she rushed to arrange a medical air flight to an El Paso hospital, 200 miles from home. There was no time for me to ask questions, not of Steve, not of the doctors. No time to process any of the emotions clashing about in my mind and heart as he was wheeled away on a stretcher to an awaiting ambulance.

I had to deal with what to do next, which was to drive back home, pack up a few things, and then drive to El Paso.

I went through the motions of functioning, gathering my computer, throwing clothes in a suitcase, closing up the house, while my thoughts and feelings were a scrambled mess. I was drowning in a wave of confusion and denial.

"This can't be happening!"

I couldn't even manage to tell my friends the truth as I stopped at their home on my way out of town. I needed support and a few hugs, but I wasn't ready to say CANCER. Instead, I said, "I don't know! I don't know! They're taking him to El Paso."

It was November 2013.

I arrived at the hospital to find Steve in the ER, still awaiting admission. Apparently, they needed financial information, but at least they had given him some relief from his pain. Finally, getting him settled into his room in the Oncology ward, we were told that he would need surgery to insert stints into his kidneys, but as it was the Thanksgiving weekend, we had to wait until Monday.

Insisting that I not hold vigil in his room, Steve sent me off to my hotel room, where I made a few phone calls before totally falling apart. First, a call to my daughter, who immediately responded, "I'm coming. You need me." Living on the other side of the country, she had originally intended to visit her grandfather for the holiday weekend. I didn't resist, but numbly accepted her support and changed my hotel room to a double. After she arrived the next day, we took turns staying with Steve.

In the turmoil of crisis, my insides churned like the cycles of a washing machine. Inundation, agitation, spin, repeat. At the hospital, I held my emotions at bay, trying to understand incoming medical updates, grappling with financial concerns, shielding Steve and my daughter from my anguish. Dealing only with what was directly in front of me while pretending that death wasn't coming. It couldn't possibly be coming! I wouldn't let it!

Alone in the hotel room, I sobbed and wailed like a toddler having a tantrum. "It's not fair!"

Full of self-pity and fear, I pleaded with Spirit guides, known and unknown, for Steve's cancer to be cured, or at least managed. I couldn't fathom losing him, not now. Not ever!

Finally, I had a good life with a good man, and this just *couldn't* be happening. I reeled in denial, convincing myself that this whole ordeal was some kind of test being thrust upon me.

Everything was so out of my control. Steve was suffering, mostly silently, and I was powerless. I was frantic and impatient with the hospital staff, trying to get answers. The nurses couldn't tell me much and his doctors were elusive. Their visits to Steve would occur between six and seven in the morning, before I arrived at the hospital, and I didn't know how to reach them during the day. Because he had arrived in the hospital from the Emergency Room, Steve didn't have a regular Oncology doctor to consult or manage care but was instead assessed and treated by whichever doctor was on shift each day.

Steve and I rarely had clear conversations about his condition as he was either in too much pain or too medicated, and we were usually focused on his immediate needs. Steve may have been given a prognosis. If so, the details were not relayed to me.

Only once did I catch his surgeon who told me, "I can't cure him, but I can control it." Before I could ask any questions, he hurried off to his next patient. No time frame, no discussion of options or odds. I pinned my hopes on that one comment.

Each day of that first week, there was a different intense development; too much too fast! Three surgeries in five days. Though the surgeries were necessary to alleviate his blocked kidneys and to slow the rapid development of his cancer, Steve hardly had time to recover from one surgery before he was scheduled for another.

I held his hand as he bravely faced being wheeled away to the operating room and was at his side waiting for him to wake up after each surgery, I tried to be as strong as he was. I could only pretend.

Chapter 6

Asking For Help

Even with so much pain and duress, Steve was somehow able to maintain an even temperament and his usual ridiculous sense of humor. During one rather intense episode of needing a catheter, he told the nurse, "I'll need an extra long one! Ha ha ha!" She just blushed and shook her head in amazement.

Even after their shifts, nurses would come to visit him. They told stories of other patients being mean or racist, and thanked Steve for being kind. "Why wouldn't I be? You are doing everything to take care of me and I am totally dependent upon you!"

There was a woman who came to clean the room daily, who sang beautiful songs in Spanish while she went about her tasks. Whenever she entered, no matter who else was visiting, Steve would wave us into silence so that he could fully immerse himself and be soothed by the angelic resonance of her voice.

He told her, "Genevieve, you are the most important person here."

Through his illness and an extensive course of medical treatments, Steve never expressed fear or feeling sorry for himself. He was extremely grateful to those who rose to the occasion to support him. He could hardly believe that so many people had immediately and generously donated to a *GoFundMe* campaign set up by one of our friends. From his hospital bed, he would put his hand on the stacks of cards received, giving him strength to "not leave the planet." I think it was the first time in his life that he embraced how truly loved he was.

His illness brought a rare occasion for both of us: a need to ask for help. We were each used to being self-sufficient, and most often, being the ones who helped others. It's remarkable how readily a crisis makes a person set aside their resistance to receiving!

The lady in the hospital finance department and I became friends, as I made regular trips to monitor fees charged, and in hopes of some eventual leniency. We cried together, hugged, and shared about our families and love relationships. At our last meeting, the morning of Steve's discharge, she reduced our $240k bill to $30k. It pays to be nice!

When we needed to find a short-term residence in El Paso, for Steve's scheduled two months of radiation treatments, our Marfa friends put out the word and found us a sweet guest cottage behind a home in a beautiful residential neighborhood. The couple who lived there were very kind and accommodating.

While I was getting everything organized for Steve to leave the hospital, my daughter managed to have a hospital bed arranged for and delivered to our new 'home.' Finally, after three weeks of sharing my hotel room while Steve was in the hospital, it was time for her to return to her own life. I was so grateful she had come, for sharing the emotional load, for researching and explaining medical terminology, for her ability to think clearly when I couldn't, and especially, for showing me the wise and wonderfully patient woman she had become. I also knew it meant the world to Steve that she loved and cared for him as she did.

Steve underwent radiation treatments two or three times a week. The goal was mostly to alleviate the pain and deterioration of bone in his pelvic region, which it did, but not without some adverse side effects.

A client of mine volunteered to do *Healing Touch* energy work with him. Modifying her techniques to work remotely, these sessions were conducted over the phone. Even so, there was not much talking. Elizabeth would start by asking how he was doing, then tune in to his body, call in cosmic energy and guides, and ask for their help.

At the start of each treatment, Steve was often in a state of pain, nausea, agitation, and anxiety. Within a half hour, he would shift into a state of calm and grace. While on the phone, I would hear him sigh gently, "Ahhhh. This is amazing."

In my observation, it appeared as if he was being lifted out of his human suffering and into a higher dimension of bliss. We didn't have any delusions that she was healing him of cancer, but he told me, "I don't know how I would be able to cope without her."

I am forever grateful to Elizabeth for her immensely valuable time and energy, which she continued to volunteer throughout Steve's illness.

After several months in El Paso for treatment, we finally returned home to Marfa. Steve spent much of his time sitting in a chaise lounge on the back patio, enjoying the sunshine and expansive views of the open high desert range. Aside from doing occasional client sessions, my time was filled with trying to prepare healthy food at a moment's notice, keeping up with phone calls to friends and family, researching cancer information online, managing the piles of medical bills, and trying to stay sane.

We set up a hospital bed in our large bedroom. Even though we both missed sleeping together, he could hardly stand to be touched because his whole body was too fragile, too vulnerable with pain. At one point, he managed to move himself back to our shared bed and beckoned for me to come and let him hold me because, "I know you need comforting too."

ASKING FOR HELP

Chapter 7

Hindsight

For the next few months, we seemed to be in a holding pattern and I finally had a breather from daily crisis mode. I started to come to terms with the severity of his condition. At the same time, I was torturing myself with remorse that I had missed the clues to his developing illness. If only I had been paying better attention.

For the last year or so, Steve had been lacking in his usual vigor and stamina, which he attributed to aging, or what he called, "The Dwindle." I hadn't questioned his early retirement from building, nor the way he dragged, physically and mentally, when moving into our beautiful new home a year ago.

Friends had reported to me that he looked especially sad while I was on my most recent summer work trip to Japan. The changes happened so gradually,

I hadn't noticed that Steve was getting very skinny and losing his usual robust attitude.

In early October, he was taking down his art show at The Marfa Book Company gallery and tripped on the curb while carrying a glass-framed print to the car. Witnesses reported a spectacular lunge, amazed that Steve had managed not to fall. Apparently, he was determined not to drop or damage his artwork. What he'd told me was that he'd felt a searing pain in his left butt cheek and assured me that it was probably nothing more than a pulled hamstring.

We found out later that the cancer had deteriorated his pelvis to the point that the muscle strain had pulled off a piece of the bone. At the time of the injury, he had minimized the severity of any ongoing pain and blew me off when I suggested he get an x-ray.

In the time between that tripping accident and his cancer diagnosis, Steve limped around with a cane and took Ibuprofen regularly, but hardly drew anyone's notice to his pain. He was determined to visit our friends in Juarez, Mexico and to travel south through the Chihuahua Desert to a ceramic artist's village near the ancient ruins of Paquime. There was a specific ceramist he wanted to meet, one of many who were making works with the same processes as their ancestors.

Steve withstood the many hours-long car ride without complaint, only requesting the occasional stop to stretch. After a delightful exchange with the local ceramists, we walked through the ruins of the ancient civilization and even joined the local townspeople for their annual Sotol Festival. This parade on foot involved following a donkey carrying a keg of Sotol, which is a distilled cactus alcohol much like tequila. Steve enjoyed himself freely and didn't avoid any of the activities that would have signaled a major medical problem.

Much later, when we were discussing how well he hid the seriousness of his physical symptoms and suffering, I asked how he had managed. "I just set the pain outside of myself." He made no explanation of how he could do such a thing, as if his ability to do so were commonplace.

On our return from Mexico, he developed symptoms of a kidney infection and I assumed he was over-using Ibuprofen. For several weeks, he refused my pleas to see a doctor. It wasn't until his pain was severe and his closest friends convinced him of the seriousness of his condition that he finally agreed to let me take him to the hospital.

In hindsight, I find it hard to believe that he thought his trouble was only a pulled hamstring and kidney infection. Rather, I'm guessing he was aware of his illness, but was trying to avoid it for a number of reasons. Steve had a scientific and inquisitive mind, and all he had to do was look up his symptoms to suspect he had cancer.

Or maybe, he *had* seen a doctor. I'll never know for sure. Once when I was bemoaning not catching the problem sooner, he seemed resigned, "Well, then they would have started cutting on me sooner. I would have missed out on so much."

What he would have missed out on was a prolific production of artwork that summer, our trip to Mexico, and several local gatherings with friends. Steve's show at the Marfa Book Company included new paintings and prints, entitled *Crossover*. At the time, we both agreed that the name was a fitting description for the blending of technology and imagination which was thematic in his art. Now, the title seems more apropos to his state of being, of what was to come.

Perhaps he knew, if only subconsciously.

Early that fall, Steve had been asked to create visual imagery for a spoken-word video, entitled *Heaven Is All Goodbyes*. The poet was the son of a black man murdered by police in Chicago in the late 1970s, telling the story of the poet and his brother driving the father's ashes home.

The content of the story struck a chord with Steve because he had lived in Detroit during that time. Steve talked to me about reviewing his own experience of fighting for social justice during the Vietnam War era. He seemed to be processing much of what his life had encompassed.

HINDSIGHT

Chapter 8

Facing the Worst

We were home in Marfa for the spring of 2014, as for now, his condition was stable, though not much improved. He was told to rest, gain weight, and "wait and see." Steve seemed resigned and yet also willing to try anything that had a reasonable possibility of a remedy.

He researched alternative treatments utilizing food as medicine, which I did my best to implement, even though more dietary limitations made it even harder to keep his weight up. I would hurry to make something he requested, but often, by the time I delivered his meal a brief while later, he could no longer stomach eating.

Each time we embarked on one of these nutritional 'cures,' I cycled through the emotional ups and downs of hope, followed by disappointment and despair. There was no improvement.

By the summer, his cancer markers were again on the rise and his doctors recommended a return to traditional treatment. We were told that at this advanced stage, the cancer probably wouldn't be affected by Chemotherapy. He went through it anyway because his oncology doctor could only prescribe a promising new drug after a patient underwent a sequence of *ineffective* Chemo.

The Chemo was indeed ineffective and made Steve even weaker and sicker. When finally he was eligible and taking the new drug, instead of improvement, his adrenals immediately began to shut down, and that treatment came to an abrupt halt, along with our hope for a medical remedy.

Cancer was bad enough, but putting Steve through useless treatment was like standing by and giving permission for him to be tortured by an unseen force. I know people who have been saved with Chemotherapy, but for Steve, it destroyed what little quality of life he might have been able to maintain.

As a last option, we were referred to a specialist in San Antonio who was researching new cancer treatments. After a very long drive, we met with the first doctor to talk straight with us. He said that with

Steve's advanced condition, "There is nothing more in the medical world that I can offer."

He recommended that we go home and put Steve's affairs in order, including saying goodbye. However, he also made the comment, "Miracles have been known to happen."

In my life, I had witnessed and even participated in a few miracles, and I was counting on one now.

Many years ago, a dear friend had been in a coma for two months with a brain injury. Her husband was desperate, and so even though he was a skeptic of spiritual things, he asked me to lead a group and "do something."

There were about thirty of us, gathered in a circle in a park. I led the intention that we all focus on how much we loved Chris, visualizing a dome of light above our heads. After a few minutes, we switched to collectively 'sending' healing energy as a pure ball of light and love, to wherever her soul could receive it.

Then we dispersed, not aware of any effect, other than we all felt more hopeful and less powerless. Within a few days, Jim called to tell me that Chris was awake. She was mentally very foggy, but still, she was able to recount having had a profound experience during her unconsciousness.

She described a group of Angels who were comforting her and leading her somewhere and that she was happy to be with them. Then she looked back and saw "all of the people who love me." She was so moved by the love she felt, she told the Angels she didn't want to leave. And then she woke up.

Love had been her miracle.

So now, for Steve, with nothing left but love and hope, we gathered our close friends in the living room. Without words, we focused on creating a circle of healing energy, holding a vision of sending love and light to Steve, clearing anything from his body that was 'not love.' We did this several times over the course of a week. The energy felt powerful while we were at it and Steve said he could feel our love coming to him from the other room.

But for Steve there was no miracle.

I felt a tremendous failure. Even my love wasn't enough. When I expressed my regret at how much he had suffered through all the ineffective treatments, he tried to reassure me.

"If we hadn't tried everything, you would always have wondered if something could have saved me."

It was true that we had tried everything. Traditional medical treatments, surgeries, radiation, chemo, alternative remedies and nutritional programs, and even energy healing. Nothing could stop the cancer.

The focus shifted to trying to keep Steve as comfortable as possible. Since his time at the hospital, his pain had been managed by slow-release morphine patches, with minimal detrimental effects. Now, he was starting to need stronger and more frequent doses to get relief from increasing pain. The higher doses drove him into a drug-induced stupor. In between doses, he would become agitated and frightened, as if he were seeing demons that were not there. Totally out of character for Steve. More like the psychosis of a heroin junkie, which I learned was a common side effect for patients on morphine.

Fortunately, we were able to supplement his opioids with a concentrated form of Cannibis Oil. With the oil, he was able to return to lower doses of morphine, while maintaining a low and manageable level of pain. His appetite returned somewhat and his whole being seemed to breathe a sign of relief.

So did mine, but only temporarily.

I was so distraught at the thought of losing him, I didn't give up the idea of a cure until the very end, when he started to say things like, "I'm getting very remote." At this point, he was refusing food, and was no longer interested in being outside of the bedroom. He spent much more time wanting to be left alone.

When he said to me, "I'm looking at my own death," I got the sense that he was not afraid of dying. He seemed ready to let go. He was also trying to get me to face reality.

Chapter 9

A Graceful Departure

Steve wasn't an outwardly spiritual person, yet he had a profound understanding of life and people. Time and time again in his life, he demonstrated a healthy balance between determination and acceptance. When he was passionate about a goal, he gave it his all. He was also realistic and knew when continuing efforts would be a waste of time and energy. In those cases, he would simply release the situation without blame or frustration and move on to the next thing.

Now, Steve was accepting his own impending death with that same grace.

Towards the end, he emanated a calm and soothing presence. Visitors would enter his room distressed and leave at peace. Even in the face of death, Steve retained a sense of humor and was delighted by my attempts to amuse him or make him laugh.

There were long periods when he would be asleep or at least not conscious. One time, as he opened his eyes, he had a far-away look of awe and a blissful smile, so I asked, "Where have you been?"

"Ahhhhh," he mused with a long, dreamy sigh, "Everywhere!"

In my client work, I had heard many stories about near-death experiences, with people recounting their varied and personal visions of what lay beyond this physical existence. I was also aware that when a person approaches their death, they may witness people waiting for them on the other side, as well as other advance notice of where they are going.

Steve seemed to be having a preview of sorts and I was exceedingly curious about what he was experiencing.

"Is it like being in a Fractal?" I asked, knowing how aligned he was with that visual concept.

"I AM a fractal!"

Wow. No further description was needed for me to understand that he had been given a taste of a future reality. With this exalted viewpoint, not only was he at peace, but he also seemed even a bit eager to leave this life and begin the adventure that would follow.

Any sadness that he expressed was not for himself, but for those who would suffer in his absence. The day before Steve died, in a sweet and frail voice he whispered to me, "I really don't want to leave you, but this Meat-Suit is toast." To hear those words helped me accept that he had stopped trying to resist death, that he had no choice but to abandon his tortured body. Which left me with no choice but to find a way to cope.

I knew that Steve was getting ready to leave his body, but still, I clung to some hope that I would not lose him completely. The notion of after-death communication was familiar to me, as well as Steve, so I brought up the subject.

"Do you think we will be able to stay connected?"

"Um-hum," he mumbled in assent.

I asked, "How?"

In a wispy voice, he advised. "Keep your antennae on." I knew what he meant by antennae, as I made a practice of 'tuning in' to connect with the Spirit realm. For me, sensing what could not be seen was a matter of intention and focus, with an openness to receiving, followed by a healthy dose of discernment. In my client work and for myself, I often received useful messages from Spirit guides, but I wanted some clarity.

I asked Steve, "How will I know it's you?" Immediately, he promised, "I'll bring you a feather."

That last night, in September of 2014, we were all there. Steve's two grown sons and my daughter gathered at the foot of his bed. I held one hand on his heart and one on his head as his labored breath mimicked that of a person climbing a mountain. His soul seemed to be working hard to break free of his used-up body, the way a butterfly struggles out of its cocoon. His eyes were closed, but his energy was intense and focused.

Somehow, I managed to put my anguish at losing him aside to be the focal point of love and support, chanting softly in rhythm with his breath. "Let go. It's okay. Let go." When his labored breathing shifted to one heavy exhale, I felt the familiar essence of his soul blow into my chest, swirl around in my heart, then rise up and out through the top of my head.

And he was gone.

Chapter 10

Signs of Life from Beyond

I left the room and broke down in sobs. It was three in the morning.

We waited until daybreak to send for the officials. After my call to them around 8:30 a.m., I stood in the kitchen with my friend, waiting for their arrival. Since our address could be hard to locate, I was holding my phone in case the mortuary folks called for directions.

By 9:45 a.m., I was a bit concerned, so I looked to see if I had missed a call. There had been no ring, but there appeared to be a new voice message, time-stamped 9:30 a.m. Odd.

Pressing 'play,' I was shocked to hear Steve's robust and cheerful voice. This wasn't the frail voice of his last weeks, but the bold and enthusiastic voice I knew and loved, the one I had heard at our first meeting.

"Well, Hey there!" (pause) "And by the way, I LOVE you!" This, followed by a roll of joyful laughter. "Bye now!"

I listened again in disbelief. I was sure I'd never heard that message before. Where had it come from?

I immediately shared the recorded message with my friend, just to make sure I wasn't imagining things in my grief and exhaustion. Checking the time stamp together, we listened several times, speechless and in tears.

Hearing his voice, I had a strong sense that Steve was letting me know that he was okay. He was no longer suffering, but I was a mess. It felt like I had a hole blown through my heart.

All my happiness was gone. It went with Steve. I wanted so much to go with him, to be where he was. The reality of our irreparable separation was brutal.

I shouted to him, nowhere and everywhere, "I don't want to be here without you!"

His phone message sparked my awareness that perhaps he really would be able to stay in touch with me. In the days immediately following, there were several odd occurrences which got my attention, even though most people would probably discount them as coincidence. I found value and meaning in what I took to be signs from the other side.

The first day after Steve's death, I was in a state of shock and despair. For so many months, I had held to a relentless belief that something would save him. I felt like a failure, as if I wasn't good enough, as if I should have done more. I had so many regrets, so much I wished I could have done better for him. I went out on the porch to sit in his favorite place overlooking miles of high desert.

At the foot of his chair was a small dead bird, showing no visible signs of its demise. It seemed that I couldn't escape death. But I was also reminded that death is a part of nature, that it just happens sometimes. I would have to find a way to accept Steve's.

Waking up in the bedroom I had shared with Steve was hard. Each morning would slam me back into the reality of loss. For many months, he had occupied a corner of our room in his small hospital bed. Now that spot was empty. Empty of the hospital bed. Empty of Steve. I was alone. Yet, for three mornings in a row, I woke to the clamoring of a large bird up on the trellis which framed the bedroom window.

The first time it appeared, I could hardly believe the sight of a roadrunner perched six feet above the ground staring intently straight at me, shuffling about, and tapping its beak on the glass. As soon as I paid attention to it, the bird froze with its gaze still on me, but only for a moment before jumping down and scurrying off.

Roadrunners are ground-dwelling birds, except for when they build nests for their young a few feet up into a small bush. They prefer to avoid humans. In fact, we had never before seen one on our property, nor in town, but only out in nature.

To have a roadrunner so close, and so pointedly intent upon getting my attention, definitely GOT my attention.

The second time I awoke to the roadrunner, I was still surprised, but I greeted it. "Hello, Steve." As soon as I did so, it once again froze, holding its gaze on me, then jumped down and ran off.

For three days, I embraced the bird's appearance as a game of sorts, though a meaningful one. I was tantalized by the notion that perhaps Steve's soul could come through a creature of nature and with such unusual and comical behavior. If so, it was fitting that he would present as a roadrunner, rather than a more commonly seen bird, as the roadrunners we had seen while visiting Big Bend National Park had delighted me to no end, and also because a roadrunner was so totally out of place here, at our home in town.

After those three days, the roadrunner no longer woke me from the trellis. Instead, I occasionally spotted it down by the peach tree below Steve's studio, a favorite place of his. The roadrunner's unusual presence was also reported around town, at the homes of several of Steve's friends.

Whether or not there was any reality to associating Steve with the roadrunner, doing so helped me feel that his energy was still present, that his essence lived on, and *that* gave me hope for my own future.

In addition to the message on my phone and the antics of the roadrunner, I also began 'hearing' Steve's voice in my mind. Like someone calling from the other end of the house, the sound of his voice was distant, but could be understood.

The first instance of his verbal guidance from beyond came within days of his death.

I got news that a relative of his, whom I had never had any contact with was making plans to travel across country to Marfa. Steve had not been close to her and had not received any concern, nor even a Get-Well card from her during his illness. Without contacting me directly or offering any condolence, she had told other family members that she had "a right to come and see where her uncle lived!"

I panicked at the thought of a stranger rifling through Steve's studio, perhaps attempting to bulldoze me in my vulnerable state. I didn't have the strength to deal with anyone coming out of nowhere and making demands. I just wanted to be left alone to process an overload of emotions.

I looked up into the big West Texas sky and implored, "Steve! What am I going to do?"

"RUUUUUN!" was the immediate word that popped into my mind! I laughed with relief.

Maybe it was my wishful thinking or my own inner wisdom, but the word seemed to be in Steve's voice and was just like what he would say! He always had a unique style of humor in challenging situations and was never one to accommodate other people's bad behavior.

Feeling reassured, I thanked him, and following his advice, I put a stop to her visit.

I was grateful for these signs, which gave me a bit more strength than I would have had otherwise. Part of me anticipated that my ability to have a connection with Steve would be short lived, as it had been with Mom after her death. I resolved to appreciate these special occurrences for as long as they might last.

SIGNS OF LIFE FROM BEYOND

Chapter 11

Goodbye Ceremonies and Shooting Stars

There was no formal memorial immediately following his death. Neither Steve nor I were traditional, and we were both adverse to the idea of a bunch of people sitting around weeping. Besides, I wasn't up for that kind of public grieving, as there was a tendency for people to look to me for strength and solace, or ask uncomfortable questions, instead of offering me any real comfort.

Instead, I chose to honor him privately by returning to his favorite camping spot in Big Bend National Park. I made a simple placement of small rocks and leaves around a natural hole in a large flat rock as a way for me to envision him always sitting on the top of that rise, overlooking the Chisos Mountains, like an ancient Apache at peace with the land.

As I sat on the rock, I began to sing. No words; no particular song. It seemed natural to let sound come out of my mouth, much as the tears were now flowing unrestricted from my eyes.

In the wide-open expanse and solitude of this place and this moment, with a gentle breeze sweeping past me, I finally let the pain in my heart find some small escape. After a bit, I sat silently and could 'feel' an embrace of sorts come from behind me, like a cloak being wrapped around my shoulders. Instead of questioning, I allowed myself to be comforted.

This seemed to be a good time to talk to Steve, for if there was anywhere that he might be able to hear me, it would be at his favorite spot.

"I need you, Steve! What can you tell me?"

Like the soft wind, these words drifted past my ears:

"Remember our story. Tell it to others. (*Pause*) Stay with the ones who love you. There are many. (*Pause*) I will always be with you."

Somehow, in this place, and perhaps because of my strong desire and intention, I was able to receive such a meaningful message. At the time, I wasn't clear how to apply Steve's wisdom to my broken life. Looking back years later, and as my life has proceeded, his advice makes perfect sense.

In November 2014, we held a Celebration of Life gathering. No, it was a *party*! Many people from the community, as well as friends from near and far, came to exchange condolences and share stories. Several groups of local musicians played their hearts out in musical tribute to Steve and we all reveled in the grateful appreciation of having known such a remarkably wise, loving, and talented soul.

There was a slide show of photographs, gathered from multiple sources, covering the full range of Steve's life, from childhood through recent times. The snapshot images were projected on the wall behind us as a rolling backdrop for the evening.

People stood up and told amusing stories. Many spoke of Steve's kindness and the meaningful contribution that he had made in their lives. Some stories had us all laughing at Steve's ridiculous sense of humor and antics. Others revealed Steve as the culprit in harmless, but mischievous adventures.

When it was my turn to share, I announced to the crowd of friends, "Thank you for coming! You know how much Steve loved a good party. And this is a GREAT party!"

At that exact moment everyone started cheering and pointing behind me. Turning around, I was astonished to see a MOVING clip of Steve, smiling with the joy of a trickster and gesturing profanely at the crowd! The clip rolled and repeated several times before the regular slide show resumed.

With this astounding and hilarious occurrence, there seemed to be a collective release of tension, as if we were all reassured of Steve's ongoing presence. Even after death, he was somehow continuing to delight us! Later, none of the contributors to the slide show could explain the appearance of that clip, and on subsequent viewings, the clip was no longer there.

Other strange things occurred that night. The party was outdoors and occasionally, someone would point to the dark night sky and squeal, "Oooh look, a shooting star!" "There's another one!" "Oooh, that one was GREEN!"

For shooting stars to appear as green is unusual, and particularly noteworthy. Steve had been part of the early CGI animation world and loved telling his story about creating the green fire coming out of a plane in the film, *Born on the Fourth of July*. Friends in Austin, San Antonio, Chicago and New York City, all toasting Steve from afar, reported multiple shooting stars that same night. All of them green.

The gathering in November was an important way to share grief with friends and brought a satisfying sense of closure for many. For me, I continued to need a way of processing my loss. I needed something more personal and a place to go and talk with my lost best friend. The site in Big Bend was too far away for me to visit on a regular basis, so two months after the community Celebration of Life, I decided that the perfect location would be under the pear tree in our yard where Steve liked to sit.

My friend Robin and I gathered a few meaningful things and created a simple ceremony there. We dug a small hole where we first buried a shock of my hair tied with Steve's hair. Next, we spread some of his ashes. After adding a stub of charcoal from his sketching supplies, we sprinkled a dash of his tobacco.

Finally, we topped these symbolic items with a hand-sized ceramic lid that I had made especially for Steve. The ball handle of the lid was made in the shape of a ladybug, which was especially meaningful. Ladybug was another pet name Steve had given me.

Robin and I shed a few tears and tenderly pronounced, "Goodbye, Steve. We love you, forever." Then, we filled the hole with dirt, scattered a few rose petals over the area, and set a large crystal on top to mark the spot.

I would visit there often, and it brought me some comfort. Much like the time I felt Steve's presence on the flat rock in Big Bend, when I sat quietly under the pear tree, I could 'feel' a warm cloak wrapped around me. And it was there that I could most readily hear his words of love to ease the absence of his physical presence.

Chapter 12

Making Friends With Grief

I found myself in a void.

While others were able to return to their lives, with children and partners, I was now alone. Alone in my house. Alone as I moved through the world. Alone in all the daily experiences that used to be shared.

Steve was missed by many, but his absence didn't radically alter their lives. Mine was forever exploded. My best friend, my loving accomplice, my solidarity, GONE.

I had been through many other situations where the bottom suddenly dropped out of my life and I had managed to cope. During a tumultuous unraveling and divorce from an unhinged first husband, I had also dealt with a back injury which led to my loss of employment and financial stability. In that challenging situation, acknowledging the abuse that I was leaving behind in both my marriage and my job created a furious determination in me to move forward with a positive attitude for a fresh start. No looking back.

Now, losing Steve, what I was leaving behind was happiness and I couldn't apply that same strategy.

During my daughter's teenaged years, a series of crises had required heart-wrenching choices and fast action. I toughened myself up to maintain a cool head instead of being overly sentimental. In those situations, even though much was out of my control, I was at least effective in "keeping the motorboat steered away from the rocks."

Now, Steve was gone. No effort could bring him back.

More recently, I had been struck by the sudden betrayal of my siblings after Mom's death. The emotional turmoil I felt in that unfair turn of events was eased by Steve's love and support. At the time, I was actually relieved to have an end to life-long toxic relationships and moved forward with strength a sense of having been liberated.

Now, I screamed to the empty spaces, "What am I supposed to do with *this*?"

I felt utterly defeated. Grief had extinguished the spark of my spirit and wrapped me in a blanket of dull confusion. My heart was numb and my mind was scrambled.

Even small decisions seemed overwhelming. I would bounce back and forth between rooms for extended periods of time, unable to decide what to focus on for that day. I would leave the vacuuming half finished or absentmindedly step outside without knowing why. Grief also came to me urging frantic activity and fixation on unimportant tasks, which taxed my already exhausted nervous system.

A regular job would have given me some structure and socialization, but I was self-employed. In my current state of emotional disarray, I lacked the enthusiasm needed to reactivate my career as a Clairvoyant through online marketing or out-of-town events. It was only the occasional client phone session which kept me connected to my higher self.

Until I could recover and restore my own life, I sought meaningful connection where I could find it.

There were moments of respite from grief. Helping a friend with her toddler, doing office work for an artist friend, having a resident artist set up a workspace in a corner of my ceramics studio, all eased my disconnect from the world.

My loneliness had me floundering. For almost a year, I had taken care of Steve. Now that sense of purpose was gone. I couldn't stop thinking about him, and missing him, so I turned my focus to honoring his life of art.

I spent many hours pulling prints out of drawers, unwrapping canvases, looking through sketch books. Such a huge volume of beautiful creations, many from his early-20s, through his blossoming career in the 80s and 90s, most of which I had never seen before. I developed a deeper appreciation for his natural talent and brilliant innovations as I meticulously sorted and catalogued every piece.

Becoming intimate with Steve's work gave me a way of being with him. These newly discovered artworks spoke to me in their own unique voices, telling the story of Steve's evolution as an artist. Without really understanding why I was doing all of this, I stayed passionate in my purpose, as my days seemed pointless otherwise.

Serendipity appeared and I was presented with the opportunity to put together a retrospective show of Steve's art. Vicki, the gallery manager at a popular downtown hotel invited me to exhibit his work over the Christmas holiday season and we scheduled an opening for December. I was encouraged to display works in the large Ballroom in addition to the usual gallery space.

I set to the task of choosing which paintings and prints to display, deciding what to sell and what to keep. As an artist myself, I knew how to do framing and labeling for display on walls, and how to package prints for sale in racks. I compiled a mailing list, created postcards, and put an ad in the local paper. It felt good to apply my business and graphic design skills to honor Steve.

Getting everything ready in time for the opening gave me the motivation to keep moving forward and provided a way to distract myself from the pain lodged in my heart. All the while, I knew that this activity wasn't going to fill my life ongoing, but that my devotion to his life in art was part of my healing.

I could hear Steve's voice in the back of my mind, "Don't you have something of your own to do?" which is exactly what he used to say when I became overly helpful with his projects at the neglect of my own. I could chuckle at his silent voice and respond to nowhere, "Don't worry. I'm not going to be an Art Widow!"

The show ultimately was an enormous success and provided substantial finances to carry me through months of little other income. Many people came and enjoyed learning more about how Steve's talent and style had developed from beginning to end. I only wished he could have been there to witness the acknowledgment and respect he could now claim as an artist.

Once the show was over, I again found myself without focus. Since Steve's death, I knew that my time in Marfa had come to a close. Even so, I was determined not to make any major life decisions for a year. Instead, I would live with not knowing what would come next.

Trying to navigate through awkward encounters in this little town became oppressive. I was often asked, "What are you going to do now?"

I could only respond, "I've been a single woman before. I'll reinvent myself again."

Even a normal errand to the post office or grocery store, became stressful as I was often faced with inappropriate encounters. People I hardly knew would get a little too close and ask in feigned sympathy, "How ARE you?"

Once, about a month after Steve's death, friends took me out to a local music event where an older woman spewed her Catholic judgment at me, accusing rather than asking, "What are you doing here?" Was I not allowed to have any joy until some unspecified time of suffering was endured?

I felt all eyes on me. Perhaps, they meant well, but the attention of semi-strangers was not helpful.

What *was* helpful were my true friends, the ones who invited me to dinner or included me in social activities, the women who gathered for a weekly "*Stitch & Bitch*" knitting group, telling stories and laughing. I am grateful for the people who treated me more normally, who allowed me to be whatever I needed to be in any moment.

And what helped me the most was an invitation to visit my lifelong friends living in Montana. They fed me and included me, and loved me. We sat together on their couch and cried. Though they had only met Steve once, they wanted to hear my stories. With their authentic tenderness and support, I was able to let go of presenting as if I was okay for other people. I shed big tears and broke through the outer layers of containment that kept my heart festering. I regained hope that this cloud of pain would not always be with me. They may have saved my life, and I do not say that to be dramatic.

In addition to taking an emotional toll, the many months of caretaking and putting my own needs aside had resulted in unhealthy weight loss and fatigue. The normal activity of going for a brisk walk would trigger my heart to race in panic and urgency. Though the crisis was behind me, my body responded like I was still on alert, tending to Steve in his illness. When it was time for sleep, even though I was often exhausted, I found myself wired in a state of hyper-vigilance. Anxiety coursed through me, sustaining a panic reaction which was lingering long after any danger had passed.

I began to take better care of my physical body, with nutrition and vitamins, but my mental state was a ferocious mess. Like a freight train running in a loop, my overactive mind kept passing by the same routes and stopping at the same stations: Blame, Remorse, Survivor Guilt, Self-pity.

For some people, using traditional meditation techniques is a way to achieve calm, but I simply couldn't concentrate. The ache in my heart was driving all of my thoughts, leading nowhere. I was no closer to accepting my new reality, no closer to seeing a way out.

To keep my mind from swirling aimlessly, I turned to writing in my journal, a practice that had been therapeutic for me in the past.

Journal entry April 2015:

My dear Steve,

I miss you fiercely, in waves. Sometimes, like the gentle lapping of calm water on the soft sand of a lake shore. Other times, like the rhythmic clunking on the side of a little boat making progress through choppy waters. But mostly, impossible to ignore, like the angry surf of an ocean storm smashing and grinding against already weathered rocks.

Journal entry June 2015:

Now that you're gone, where do I put my love and devotion?

I know how to banish the memory of love lost in a break-up. I've done it countless times.

But what do I do with the memory of you?

Do I remember you, or try to forget you?

Do I live in the details and memories, or do I leave you behind?

How do I honor you, and us, without losing me, without living in the past?

How much do I hold onto?

I wish you could tell me.

But you're gone.

Chapter 13

Healing A Broken Heart

People talk of heartache or a broken heart, and now I knew what they meant. Emotional pain would manifest physically, like a boot stomping on my chest, making it hard to take a deep breath. My heart felt as if there were a gaping wound, like something actually had been torn loose.

I traveled to Tokyo, Japan that summer, continuing with the workshops and client sessions I had been doing for several years. The staff treated me with extra compassion and kindness, which was helpful as I found myself having more difficulty coping with the challenges of being in a foreign country. Previously, my eyes had viewed the unknown with delight, while I learned how to navigate the subway, buy groceries, and read menus. Now, I felt more like a small child, vulnerable and needing someone to hold my hand through these tasks.

Every activity took much more energy than on previous trips and I easily became overwhelmed around crowds of people. Though I presented as normal to others, I was still emotionally raw and sensitive on the inside.

My friend and interpreter, Fukiko, suggested that I might find some value in attending a Homa Fire Ceremony, as was practiced daily at the Fukigawa Fudo Temple in Tokyo. Over many years, I had often practiced my own version of a fire ceremony, by writing on a small piece of paper whatever unhealthy belief or pattern I wished to release, and then burning it in a fire. I wasn't sure what to expect in Japan, though I was open to the experience. I learned later that the use of fire during the ceremony at this temple symbolized the wisdom of the Buddha, burning away the root of suffering for the participants.

Inside the large temple, we all sat on the floor in front of a stage-like platform. Flanked by huge Taiko drums on tall stands was the large square fire-pit, where the main priest sat to tend the fire and lead the ceremony. Other priests in red robes moved about chanting in Japanese, and the audience added their voices, creating a background cadence which was accentuated by powerful loud drumming and the occasional blowing of a long horn.

The combined vibration moved into my body through the wooden floor, resonating at an intensely primal level. There was much happening that I didn't understand, as I sat watching the younger priests waving ceremonial staffs through the flames.

Even so, the power of the fire ceremony had a visceral effect on me. The rhythmic chanting and the deep booms of the drums were shaking loose the pain lodged in my heart.

Lulled into a semi-trance state, I closed my eyes and had a vision of Steve's face appearing upside-down in front of mine. "I'm up here now!"

In the flash of an instance, I sensed his essence reaching a long arm down to me, grabbing the invisible cord which was attached at my heart and then connecting the loose end to 'somewhere up there,' where he was. I immediately felt a profound shift deep within me; the comfort and stability of his love replacing the anguish of our separation which had until then held me in a constant state of distress.

In my spiritual practice and teaching program there is a concept of energy cords. These unseen cords between two people serve as an energy connection to each other while in physical bodies. The heart cord is especially valuable as a way to share loving feelings, even when not in each other's physical presence.

I hadn't realized that when one person dies, there is a tearing of that cord. Since Steve's death, the cord that had once united us was shredded and flailing around in search of him. I hadn't acknowledged the energetic wound to my heart until it was healed.

As people were dispersing after the ceremony, I sat in awe of my experience, and yet I was compelled by a sense of urgency to go outside into the open air. Standing on the grand entrance stairs, I faced a stripe of open blue sky, flanked by tall buildings lining both sides of the long city street leading to the temple.

Coming straight towards the temple, flying directly in the center of that line of blue sky was a large, graceful bird. Fukiko joined me outside on the steps just in time to witness a crane flying with grace and power, directly over the temple, in downtown Tokyo!

Not hiding her amazement at this rare and unexpected sight, my friend explained the multiple symbolism of Crane in Japanese culture.

Crane represents a lifelong married couple. Crane carries the souls of the dead to paradise and is also a symbol of longevity, loyalty, strength, and hope. I could absolutely relate to that symbolism and to the significance in my life. At the same time, it was not lost on me that though Crane is associated with a couple, this one was on its own, as I was now.

HEALING A BROKEN HEART

Chapter 14

100 Messages

Throughout the first year after Steve died, just about every morning, I would wake up with a short phrase present in my mind. I'm not sure where these words came from, though there was a similarity to what Steve might say and a resonant sound of his voice. The sentiments seemed to specifically address whatever aspect of my loss I was currently struggling with.

When I felt overwhelmed, I heard, "Just for today, take a breather." Or "What can you set aside until later?"

When I was dwelling on my loss, stuck in despair, with the idea that my life was ruined and I'd never be happy again, I heard, "No matter what life feels like now, something good will come of this." "Envision your beautiful life five years from now." And "Instead of focusing on what is no more, imagine what you are free to do now.'"

Many days, I was at a loss about what steps to take for my future. Once I heard, "Start to listen to that small inner voice that tells you of your dreams." Another time, "Pleasure is the food that gives you strength to keep going."

More often than not, I woke from restless sleep feeling discouraged and self-critical. On those days I received encouragement. "You are doing so much better than you think you are." "It is safe for you to have a weak moment." And "You will get through this."

Being in a state of grief and depression, it was easy for my mind to ruminate over situations and relationships from my past that increased my negative focus. Memories of happy times and successes seemed to have receded far away into a dark corner.

On those mornings, I received reminders like: "Focus on your strengths and resources rather than your weaknesses or mistakes of the past." "Only hold onto things that bring you love and comfort, not memories of pain." And "Your mistakes measure your learning, not your value."

When I was feeling inundated with the well-meaning but unhelpful advice of others, I would hear, "What works for another may be different from what will work for you." Or "Follow the ones who are out the other side of what you are going through, not the ones who are stuck."

No matter what my state of mind, these words of wisdom served to lift me up and give me a more positive perspective for the day. I wrote the phrases on post-it notes and stuck them on my desk, bathroom mirror, and refrigerator. These well-placed reminders kept me from wallowing.

Maybe the thoughts came from Steve. Maybe the ideas came from my guide or my own higher wisdom. Whatever the source, receiving these messages helped me feel supported and encouraged.

After a period of four or five months, I had gathered over 100 messages. Each of the phrases had come to me at the perfect moment, and immensely improved my attitude and ability to move forward. I started to view these words as having potential value for other people who were also going through a rough time and eventually published a card set entitled *Permissions – 100 Days of Encouragement.*

100 MESSAGES

Chapter 15

Surprise Appearance, Extraordinary Guidance

I knew that I wouldn't stay in Marfa.

Many of my closer friends had already moved away, and now without Steve, there really wasn't much there for me. Also, it felt like I was wearing 'the widow's mark.'

When Steve was alive and we would show up at a coffee shop, restaurant, or gathering, our presence was greeted with joyful enthusiasm. Now that he was gone, when I walked into a room, the others were immediately reminded of Steve's absence and the mood would drop like a lead weight. I didn't want to be that dark cloud. I knew that I should move on, but I didn't know where to go.

I sat under the pear tree and 'heard' Steve's voice in my mind. "Marfa was *my* place. Go find *your* place."

When I moved to Marfa with Steve, everything was potential and my glorious new relationship had taken precedence over some other aspects of my life. Now, that I faced an unintentionally clean slate, I reevaluated what was important to me, so that I could envision my next perfect place.

I created a list of criteria: Mountains, trees, lakes and rivers, cooler weather; opportunities for work, spiritual community, close to an airport; social and creative activities, live music, ceramics, and dance; safe and affordable. And most of all, a place where I fit in, where I would have like-minded friends to fill my need for authentic connection.

My intention set; it was time to explore.

I scheduled some work events for October 2015, up through Colorado, with the idea of checking out Colorado Springs and the Denver area. I also planned to return to Bozeman, Montana, the home of the close friends whom I had visited after Steve's death.

The first stop on my exploration was a Body-Mind-Spirit Expo in Colorado Springs, where in addition to setting up a booth to promote my book and services, I was to present a lecture on Spirit Guides.

I entered the lecture room with three items in my hands: a small clock, my brochures, and a water bottle. I set these items in the empty space beneath the lectern and began my talk. Part way through my talk, I was explaining the idea that our Spirit Guides are soul family members who are no longer having Earthly lives, but who are helping others with their human challenges.

At this point, an audience member asked, "Can a loved one who has died be our Spirit Guide now?"

I answered, "For a time, they may connect to us with love and messages, but their influence passes. They usually move on to their own journey of healing and review on the other side. In contrast, our Spirit Guides are with us from the beginning to the end of our lives."

I gave some examples of how I had experienced Steve's presence initially, including some of the signs and strange events. With some sadness, I relayed my gratitude for Steve's help, but now, "I don't feel him so much and I think he has moved on."

At the end of my talk, I grabbed those three items from the lectern and walked to the hallway to greet people as they left the room. I handed out some brochures, answered a few quick inquiries, and returned to my table in the exhibition room. I set down the water bottle, the brochures, and the clock, and realized that I was still holding something in my left hand.

What's this?

I opened my fingers and discovered a small item that I had never seen before, a black eye-liner container. Where had this come from? I spun the bottle to read the front... *E.L.F.* My knees wobbled just a little, my heart skipped a beat, and then I smiled and sat down as the meaningful revelation sank in.

Elfman was my pet name for Steve. He was showing me, again, that he wasn't gone.

I had sort of given up on talking to Steve for guidance, so the notion that his spirit hadn't abandoned me brought a surge of joy to my heart. That bottle of *E.L.F.* Eyeliner would be my reminder that I could still count on Steve for a bit of magic.

My antennae were back on!

I knew that decisions were mine to make, but I now pictured Steve riding along on my shoulder, like an imaginary friend, to give me a thumbs-down or nod of approval as I searched for my new home.

Colorado Springs had some dance activities, and some ceramics, but nothing very exciting. In fact, kind of bland. I didn't discount it totally, but moved on to explore Denver, where I had set up some bookstore events.

The Denver dance group was too large and seemed sort of showy. The dancers there weren't very friendly or welcoming, but instead of feeling left out or rejected, I simply recognized, "Okay. Not my people."

Colorado seemed to have work potential, with the worthwhile connections I had made at the Expo and other events, but I didn't get the sense that this was where I was to live.

Heading north, the next place for me to check out was Bozeman, Montana.

I had known Joe first, in college. He felt more like a brother than just a friend, someone I could always be my true self with, someone I totally trusted. After college, when I met his new girlfriend, Lauri, she and I immediately became friends. Together, the three of us had wild fun in our early twenties, and then bonded at even deeper levels as Lauri and I assisted at the birth of each other's children.

Even though we hadn't always stayed in touch through the years, I always knew I could count on them. We had stayed in touch by phone and turned to each other when life got tough. Better family than family.

These were the friends who had reached out to me immediately after Steve's passing and invited me to come to them for some comfort, which I had done in the spring.

Now I was back in Bozeman, to see if the place which my dear friends loved to call home might also be a place for me.

Joe and Lauri threw a party, and I met their friends, as well as reconnected with their two children who were now grown. Everyone was eager to engage and genuinely encouraging of my idea to move to Bozeman, with suggestions of fun things we could do together and affirmation that there would be interest in my Clairvoyant profession in this community.

I felt the welcome mat being placed before me and I thought, "How nice it would be to have a ready-made family and social group!" Other times when I had moved to a new area, it had taken at least a year to make close friends and establish local clients. This time, I really needed the immediate support that was being offered – a soft spot to land.

The mountains and rivers were stunningly beautiful, a refreshing change from the dry sparse desert. I explored ceramics opportunities and discovered a community center for classes and studio time. Next to look for dance. Nothing apparent, but as I scoured the listings on yoga studio websites, I found something that looked promising. *Ecstatic Dance: Sundays at 11:00. All Welcome.*

Walking up a flight of stairs inside the old brick building, I remembered to talk to Steve. "If Bozeman is the right place for me, show me a sign."

After taking off my shoes, I stepped into the dance area and crossed the large wooden floor towards the small group gathered beneath giant plate glass windows. The sunlight was shining so brightly through the windows that at first, I didn't notice, but then I was in awe. The entire wall was decorated with feathers stuck into the bricks!

The group greeted me with authentic delight, and after smiling and dancing together, we gathered again on the floor. One young girl shared that she had recently been given a special Eagle feather by one of her native elders, and that today she had felt a strong urge to bring it to add to the wall. As she stood to do so, I couldn't help the tears of joy that trickled down my cheeks.

When it was my turn to share, I told of my quest for a new home after the death of my soul mate. I told of his ongoing communication and my request for a sign. I told of how meaningful the feathers on the wall were, relaying that Steve had promised, "I'll bring you a feather."

Now there were others with leaking eyes, and smiles. Almost as one voice, the group cooed, "Oooh, we hope you move *here*!" And I believed them.

Returning to Joe and Lauri's home, and recounting my experience at the dance studio, I reported, "I think Bozeman wins!" They both joyfully responded, "Yay! We were hoping you'd say that, but we didn't want to pressure you. Yay!" Their heartfelt response was all I needed to validate my choice and let me know I was already home.

Chapter 16

My Move, and Mysterious
Moving Things

Once the decision to move to Bozeman was made, I returned to Marfa and started unraveling the life that Steve and I had built there. I had relocated many times before, and I knew how to gather up my important belongings and leave behind what could be easily replaced at my new home. That task wouldn't take long, and I was excited to be envisioning a new future for myself.

I wasn't the least bit sentimental about leaving the desert or the small-town mentality. Now that I had been reassured that Steve's essence would go with me, I no longer felt emotionally attached to our house. Leaving the place where we had lived would be easy, but dealing with Steve's belongings, the thought of that project immobilized me like a wave of mud.

What should I do with his clothes; the white linen shirt that I had sewn for our wedding, the silk kimono jacket I brought from Japan, his favorite straw cowboy hat? And his studio? I was overwhelmed at the thought of dismantling the studio that still reverberated with the creative vibrations of Steve's inventive mind.

How would I manage, in the ever-present silence of his absence, to go through all of his precious belongings feeling like a snoop or a thief? And what would I do with the decades of accumulated art supplies for painting, printmaking, drawing, and ceramics, and more recently, his 16mm film equipment?

As an artist myself, there were a few things I would keep. I would cherish using his favorite brushes and pens, the large pads of paper, and the empty canvases. I intended to learn how to work with the bags and jars filled with raw material Steve used to make ceramic glazes. I looked forward to wearing his painting apron, imprinted with multi-colored layers of his handprints, to make me feel close to him again. All the other art supplies would have to find new homes.

And there was more. What about the enormous collection of tools and materials he had accumulated for his building projects?

Outside Steve's art studio, the side yard looked like a salvage yard. There were bins filled with electric wires and plumbing fixtures, barrels of thin wood poles and pipe, ladders and sawhorses, stacks of window glass, and multiple piles of lumber.

In addition to a shelf filled with unused and archaic camping equipment, his detached storage shed housed enough tools and supplies to stock a small hardware store. I had no idea what most of it was for. There was even an enclosed trailer filled with a neatly organized variety of fine mahogany trim leftover from a window job. It seemed he never threw anything away!

I sat outside under the pear tree defeated by despair and overwhelm.

Steve had established himself as somewhat of a mentor to a group of younger men in Marfa. He was held in high esteem for his years of experience and knowledge in all aspects of art and building, as well as his ability to listen and give sage advice on their personal matters. Fortunately for me, several of these friends came to my rescue. They were able to identify and organize everything, and I was happy to let them have first pick at whatever they wanted.

Once many of his tools were sold or given to these friends, I assumed the next step would be a community yard sale. Instead, our friend Daniel offered a reasonable price for all that was left, including the trailers, with the idea that he would keep what he could use, and haul away the rest. He wisely anticipated, "You don't want a bunch of strangers poking around in Steve's stuff."

I hadn't even considered the emotional consequences of a public sale, so I was grateful to have the task complete. But I did make Daniel promise that he wasn't allowed to die and leave his own wife to deal a similar burden!

Next, I faced the challenge of finding a new home for Steve's beloved Airstream. Much as I knew how special it was, as a vintage model still in decent original condition, I was also sure that I had had all the good times I was going to have in it. Without Steve, what was once a place of love and joy and adventure was now a shell, a reminder of loss, and a burden to maintain.

Almost like finding a new home for a pet, I was determined that the Airstream go to people who would love and care for it as Steve did. I began the quest for the right buyer.

The first prospect was a couple from Austin who were visiting Marfa and came to look. The minute I met the trendy young woman, clearly out of place in her heels and long white gown, manicured nails, and perfectly styled hair, I was resistant. Scanning the inside, she started squealing with excitement, in a fake little girl voice.

"Oooh! This'll be so CUUUUTE when we gut it and paint the inside white for an AirBnB in our backyard!"

I felt myself getting a little nauseous, knowing that Steve would NEVER want his precious Airstream to meet with such disrespectful treatment.

Before I had the chance to say anything to dissuade them, the sky had suddenly turned ominous with dark clouds and the sound of quickly approaching thunder. In a heartbeat, the woman freaked out at the threat of a lightning storm and quickly whisked her husband into their rental car. Off they went, never to be heard from again.

I stood in the downpour, getting drenched and laughing at the sky. "Thank You, Steve!"

The second prospective buyer assured me that they wanted the Airstream for travel with their young family. That use felt more in harmony with Steve, so I was optimistic of a real sale. I greeted them in our driveway late one Saturday afternoon.

They loved the Airstream, and all seemed in alignment until we discovered that the electric hook-up cord, used to attach brakes and lights to the tow vehicle, had been cut from the trailer. Very weird, as the Airstream had been securely parked in our fenced lot. The town's only auto supply store was already closed, not to open until Monday morning.

Their original intention had been to return home that night, towing the trailer with them on an eight hour drive to East Texas. Even without the hook-up, they still wanted to take the Airstream, but I was adamant against their protests.

"I'm not going to let anyone drive such a long distance at night without brakes or tail lights."

Another set of disappointed buyers left Marfa without the Airstream. Once more, I looked to the sky and talked to Steve. "Okay. Not them either, huh?"

A few weeks later, the Airstream found a most fitting home. A young couple, wonderful friends of both mine and Steve's, let it be known that they were looking for an Airstream to live in while they remodeled their old adobe house in Marfa. They had not been aware that Steve's Airstream was for sale, so were delighted when I offered it to them.

No storms, no problems. There were no obstacles as they moved the Airstream to its new home across town. In a short time, they had spruced the trailer up, tending to many of the neglected mechanical issues and took it across the country for a summer road trip.

My heart was at peace knowing that Steve would approve of the loving care his 'baby' was receiving. In fact, I suspected he had some influence in the matter!

That April, when it was time for me to go, with everything I owned packed up in the moving van, I had one more thing to do. I would be leaving the house empty, to be sold in my absence, with no plan of returning when it did.

It occurred to me that the next owners might be a little disturbed if they discovered the items that I had buried under Steve's beloved pear tree. So once again, Robin and I gathered for a short and spontaneous ceremony, with the intention for me to release and move on from this place, and also to remove anything not already taken by the earth.

We picked up the crystal which still marked the spot and gently dug into the earth expecting to hit first the ceramic ladybug lid.

Nothing!

Perhaps it had somehow shifted position? Digging all around where it had been buried, nothing! The lid was simply gone. Instead, in its place, we found something that neither of us had ever seen before.

A bronze medallion about two inches in diameter. On one side, "BLESSED WILL YOU BE COMING IN". On the reverse, "AND BLESSED GOING OUT."

I'm still kind of speechless about this. There is no reasonable explanation.

Neither Steve nor I were the type to follow illusions. We were both practical and educated, with the ability to analyze and not jump to irrational conclusions. At the same time, we were both open to the mysteries of the Universe and to the notion that there may be more going on in this world than our human perspective can understand rationally.

I had always been fascinated with the concept that synchronicity was more than coincidence, without having a need to know exactly what was going on. There were times in my life when it seemed that magic was afoot, in serendipitous meetings and lucky breaks.

Now that I was witnessing specific physical things showing up out of nowhere or being moved in some way, my ability to embrace the inexplicable was surely being stretched. Whatever was happening here was not immediately obvious or easy to understand. All I could do was wonder!

Chapter 17

Meeting In The Dreamworld

I've always been a vivid dreamer, but after Steve's death, my dreams became more intense and were often disturbing, leaving me in a cloud of deep sadness the next day. The approach of sleep time cast me into anxiety, amplifying the grief I tried to distract myself from while awake. For many months, I resisted sleeping, watching TV or movies late into the night, trying to avoid what might come in my dream world.

Night after night, Steve would appear in my dream, eyes sparkling, smiling at me. At first, I would be so relieved to see him looking healthy and happy.

And then I would get confused, "What happened? You had cancer."

Instead of enjoying him or asking him the questions that obsessed me during the day, I slipped back into the old story. I would launch into trying to take care of him, rushing to fix a meal, or suggesting we needed to make another doctor's appointment.

One time I panicked as I realized, "Oh no! I got rid of all your stuff!"

In the dreams, when I respond with alarm, reverting to my caregiver role, he makes no move, speaks no words, only looks at me with sadness and disappointment. My unresolved emotions derailed my mind, robbing me of any comfort I might have received from his appearance and yanked me back into trauma.

I remained filled with regrets and concerns that I had not been able to help him, haunted by the idea that I had done the wrong thing. And even though I longed to find Steve in my dreams, every morning, upon waking, I would have to face losing him all over again.

Another troubling dream was set in a large public place. Steve has returned and is receiving an award, which entitles him to inclusion in some sort of very important group. I am watching, but he doesn't see me. Everyone else in the group sees and connects with him, but no matter how hard I try to be acknowledged, he is inaccessible to me. I wake up frustrated and feeling left out.

After nearly a year of tortuous sleep, I had an 'Ah Hah!' realization during a meditation. My dream mind was matching my emotional havoc and triggering a trauma response in every dream with Steve.

A new idea came to me, that perhaps Steve was coming to me in my dreams, night after night, to show me that he is okay now. Maybe I was even being shown what he is experiencing on the other side.

There, wherever 'there' is, he's not sick or suffering anymore. He is surrounded by other souls; he is not alone. In his new reality, he is being applauded for all that he accomplished in his earthly life and receiving credit for the contributions that were not acknowledged when he was alive.

When I embraced this more exalted perspective, I looked forward to finding him in my dreams, eager to witness the next steps in his journey. I then stopped anticipating being thrown back into his illness and waking up disturbed.

My dreams started to improve and he didn't turn into 'sick' Steve anymore.

Steve is sitting at a table. He looks up and smiles, glad to see me. He's totally present, and we are standing face to face. There is so much joy as we embrace, though it is more a blending of energy than a physical sensation. We are both relieved to now connect in pure love, without my habitual confusion. A beautiful feeling reaches every cell of my being and remains upon waking.

Even as my dreams became lighter, my mind was still struggling to resolve many troubling thoughts. Did Steve feel like I had done enough in taking care of him? Was he okay with my choice to move away? And, when I left Marfa, would that be the end of our connection?

I began posing these questions to him before sleep, and my dreams started showing me that I could let go of these concerns.

We are back in our Marfa house. Steve is well and we are talking about when he was working really hard, in the heat. He explained, "I was baked." And I replied, "I'm so sorry you had to work so hard."

Then I was in his arms, with him stroking my hair. He said, "I can take care of myself now." A sense of relief washed over me, hearing from him that he was no longer sick or suffering, and feeling like he was still in my life.

During the dream, I had a moment of wondering why I was selling the house now that he was back with me. "Where will we go now?" Then I remembered that I was only moving because he was gone. He reassures me, "It's okay. I'll go with you."

Many of my disturbing dreams had been set in our Marfa home, the site of his sickness, the place that had now become a hollow shell without him. Maybe my memory was influencing my dreams, holding me in a state of anguish. I wondered if I could redirect my dreams.

Before sleep, I spoke to Steve, and set my intention. "Please let me find you in the dream world, somewhere other than the Marfa house."

A few days later, I dream:

Steve came to me and swooped me up in an embrace. He was laughing with love and joy as he carried me, Superman style, through the sky. "Let me show you where I am." We flew to a vast open space filled with stars and the swirl of all colors against a dark background. From the stars came the gleeful

*resonance of a hundred children giggling. I was
immersed in a pure energy, the buzzing vibration of
all life, that set me in a state of total bliss.*

I asked, "What is this energy?"

*He smiled knowingly and then, reaching out his
unreasonably long arm, grabbed a line of white light
out of nowhere and wrapped a spiraling loop around
me. "Here, take this with you!"*

I woke up happy, savoring his love and the healing influence of the white light that was still enveloping me. I knew with certainty that he was now in a beautiful place and, absolutely, no longer ill or suffering. The sweet bliss of that dream soothed my heart and diminished another layer of my sadness.

Whenever I miss him, thinking of him swirling around in the cosmic realm brings me peace. Seeing Steve among the stars reminded me of the vision that he had a few days before died. "I AM a Fractal!"

I wonder if a person's frame of reference creates an aspect of their after-life experience. Several of my clients had shared their unique versions of near-death experiences, supporting this idea.

One man, who was raised as a Christian, reported being greeted by Jesus and witnessing *The Book of Judgment*, with good deeds on one page and failings on the other. Another man had been terrified by his experience of being lost in endless fire, a reflection of his fear of punishment from a Catholic upbringing and his guilt from his pattern of abusing women.

A female client told of a lovely vacation, sitting on a lawn chair at a beach, just the break she needed from a super stressful life! And she came back from her NDE with renewed optimism and an ability to make important changes.

I suppose we only find out what's on the other side when we go there ourselves!

A month or so after the cosmic swirl dream, there was one talking to Steve on the phone. No visual imagery, only sound. A back-and-forth conversation. His voice was very clear and I could feel a connection between us as strong as all those times talking on the phone when we were first dating.

Me: Hey, Sweetie!

Steve: Well, Hey there, My Love! (sounding almost surprised)

Me: This is cool!

Steve: Yaaaaaaa. (long drawn-out tone)

Me: That energy place was really cool!

Steve: Yaaah! (laughing)

Me: How long is this going to last?

Us both laughing with our simultaneous realization: There's no way to know.

Steve: It's time for everything that's bouncing around in your head to swirl into a continuous line.

And then, as if he were being pulled away by an invisible force, *"Bye now!"*

I woke up, eyes still closed to let awareness and meaning expand into my consciousness. The sound of his voice had been a restorative balm. More than just the exchange of words, it seemed that we were also having a mind-to-mind conversation, knowing each other's thoughts instantaneously.

Many of the regrets and bitterness, the 'what ifs' that I had been dwelling on, began to soften and fade with unspoken understanding, and Steve was happy that I was finally 'getting it.'

His love and energy, delivered through the vibration of his voice, massaged the ache in my heart. We were both delighted that we had connected so profoundly through a phone call in a dream and joyful to discover that perhaps we could do so again.

Chapter 18

Cosmic Conversations

The first few years were the hardest, but I was determined to grow through my grief instead of staying stuck. I didn't believe that time by itself would heal me, and I wasn't interested in just 'moving on.' The taste of loss would forever be on my palate.

My relationship with Steve had been rich and exceptionally valuable, and I didn't want to forget him. Focusing on the love we had shared was soothing, even though the pain of his absence poked holes in my shell of comfort. I knew that in order to become whole again, I would have to find a way to assimilate all the memories, both wonderful and horrible.

Since this wasn't the first time that I had faced life crises, I knew the value of addressing trauma at all levels, mental and emotional, as well as spiritual, and physical.

My writing and journaling, as well as my other projects and client sessions kept my mind from going down a dark hole, or at least kept me from staying there. For my frazzled nervous system, I improved my diet and took lots of Vitamin B. To process my very real and intense emotions, I explored a variety of therapeutic modalities.

In traditional counseling, I could express all my darkest feelings without concern of judgment. In a series of Somatic Therapy Workshops, which use dance and music to release trauma stress out of the body, I found a way to expel some of the ugly pain trapped in my being. The group setting allowed us to support each other, and I came away from each session feeling lighter, less alone, and more hopeful.

I was starting to untangle the intricate mess that Steve's death had woven into my life.

The awareness I gained from my dreams, as well as the continual stream of bizarre signs that seemed to come from Steve, helped me have some understanding on a spiritual level, but tranquility was a long way away.

There were times when I was able to connect with Steve in meditation, and at times even have a conversation of sorts, but I suspected that I was prone to hearing what I wanted to hear. I decided to reach out to a colleague for advice and a fresh perspective.

Cherry was a professional Intuitive, one who has a special ability to connect with the Universal Consciousness. At that time, Steve was still showing up in my dreams as a sick person, which repeatedly dragged me back into feeling helpless. I was really struggling with the self-recrimination that I should have done more, that I had failed him somehow, even though I had been utterly devoted and willing to try any possible cure.

Without any knowledge of my specific concern, only knowing that my husband had died, Cherry relayed the exact reassuring message I needed.

"There was nothing you could have done differently to save him. He had an exit point. His soul had completed everything. He could have stayed for you, but that would have led to a dark existence."

"For you, it is time to do inner healing, not to move forward too fast. Regarding your trouble sleeping, and your anxiety about what will be in the dreamworld, before you go to sleep, ask for Steve's help in releasing your anxiety about his illness."

Her reassurance that I couldn't have saved him was the added clarity I needed to stop seeing Steve as a sick person in my dreams. I took her advice and asked him to come and comfort me.

That night, I dreamt...

We are in a beautiful peaceful meadow. I'm sitting on the grass and Steve is standing behind me, sticking flowers in my hair. I can feel his joy and tenderness. Simple, innocent love, connected at the heart. No suffering, no fear.

With her words, and the dream that followed, I began to sense that Steve didn't hold me accountable for how it all turned out and I started to accept the reality of his unique life journey, rather than blaming myself or feeling abandoned by him.

I began to view our relationship with a more evolved perspective. Perhaps my role for him was to be a profound love and to help him get to Marfa and the desert, where he always wanted to be.

After the clarity and advice from Cherry, I felt I had another piece of the puzzle. And yet, there were many other pieces missing. I wanted to ask Steve some hard questions, questions I might not like the answer to.

Over the course of some years, I had witnessed and facilitated the resolution and peace that a person could attain if they received completely neutral and unsolicited communication from the other side.

One example was during a client session for a man who had been fighting in the earliest Gulf Wars. As his Spiritual Counselor and using my Clairvoyant gifts, I focused on seeking the underlying emotional aspect of his resistance to moving forward with his career goals now that he was a civilian again. I began with my usual process of tuning in to one of my guides and having the man say his name three times. What came to me immediately, with a sense of urgency, were the words, "It's not your fault, Binky."

Binky? Really? I hesitated to share a message that sounded so silly, but I'm glad I did.

The man caught his breath, then broke into tears, as he disclosed that his wife's nickname for him was Binky, because he often put their baby's pacifier in his mouth to keep from losing it. Then, he told me that she and the child had been killed by a sniper when they were with him in Iraq. It all made sense.

He didn't feel like he deserved to move on or be successful, because he had encouraged their visit. In addition to the suffering of loss, he felt responsible. With this message from his wife, he was relieved of his guilt and self-hate.

Another example came to me when I was seeking a public place to meet new clients and do short readings. I had stopped in and spoken with the owner of a downtown cafe who was eager to have me set up in her place. After showing me around, she invited me to check out the upstairs office as a private area for readings. While she returned to the kitchen, I stood alone in what was once the attic of this old home. I closed my eyes to get a sense of the place. What I saw in my mind's eye surprised me, for it was the subtle image of a little blond girl, about 2 years old, just standing, waiting.

When I went back down, I asked the woman, "Who's the little blond girl in the attic?"

It wasn't that I expected her to have met this 'ghost', I just didn't know how else to share what I had sensed. At first, she looked at me dumbfounded and I thought she was going to tell me that I was a nut case. Then, I watched her shocked reaction turn into a flood of tears.

"That's my Annie, my granddaughter. She was killed in a car accident just a few months ago. I can't believe she's here."

Later, we held a ceremony helping Annie move all the way to the other side instead of staying in between worlds to make sure her grandmother was okay. Learning of Annie, feeling her love, and then releasing her, was deeply healing for my new friend.

There were other significant moments in my client work, where I was able to set my rational mind aside to bring clear and relevant messages because I had no emotional attachment to what might come.

When it came to my own situation, I was much too subjective. I knew that I would only believe the truth of a message if I heard it from a source that was reliable, yet totally unfamiliar with me and my story.

In July of 2017, I was referred to a woman who was a professional Medium, meaning that she had an ability to connect to those on the other side. Staci didn't know anything about me, not even that I had a husband who had died. Before I could ask her any of my questions, she jumped right into describing a man with curly silver-gray hair, amazing blue eyes, and a gigantic smile.

"I keep hearing him repeat, 'My Love, My Love.'"

A bit choked up and overwhelmed, I shared, "That's my husband, Steve!"

She then proceeded to tell me how much he loved me and continued with many more messages. She relayed that he knew how much I sacrificed, and that he could really help me now.

I asked her, "How?"

The answer came: "By staying connected the way you did when you were first together. Make watercolor drawings, paint in his apron, and write letters to him. Focus on remembering the energy of being intimately together. Ask for his help."

With the confidence that she was relaying what could only come from Steve, and in a desire to put to rest my last bits of unresolved regrets, I asked a few specific questions.

"Did Steve know he was sick?"

"Yes. He knew he had cancer. He was having a hard time leaving you, and he stayed as long as he could, to be valiant for you and others."

Addressing my next question directly to Steve, I had to ask, "Why did you keep your path of cancer and dying secret from me?"

"Because I knew you'd fight against that, and I knew that would make things harder for both of us. Remember at the hospital, my words 'I am so sorry for how this is going to crash your life?' Now I know, I couldn't protect you from that."

I was blown away to hear her repeat, word for word, exactly what Steve had said to me in the Emergency Room. I took his explanations to heart and felt relief, as if a heavy shroud was being lifted off me.

For me to realize that *he* knew he was sick allowed me to feel less responsible. My lack of awareness of his cancer was by *his* conscious choice, not by a lapse on my part.

For Steve to intentionally keep his illness and probability of death to himself was in alignment with how he lived his life. He always accepted his own problems without putting burdens on others.

"Anything else?"

"Just how much he loves you, and that he's trying to help you find true love again."

Chapter 19

Letters to The Other Side

Embracing the profoundly freeing messages that I received through Staci, I set to putting loss and regret in the back seat. I focused on the warm feeling of being in love, the state of being that Steve and I had shared when he was alive.

During the first years of our relationship, when we were living separately, we had learned how to send and receive the energy of each other's love. Any time we were not together, we practiced holding the essence of the other in our hearts, first by remembering, and then meditating to sustain the warm feeling.

We also cultivated our relationship by sending creative and adoring letters. Each envelope that landed in my mailbox became a treasured blessing. Every envelope that I mailed to Steve I decorated with colorful designs that flowed from my joyful heart.

To restore a sense of that glorious connection, I took up my colored pencils and watercolor paints again. I wrote poems and letters, believing that Steve would receive them somehow, just as surely as those I had once mailed. Though the words were not the joy-filled expressions of our dating time, my writing brought a sense of closeness and of being heard.

Journal entry early July 2017:

Letters to my love:

You are riding a wheel that passes by me
As I stand and watch it go by.

The force of my being is too small to catch you,
To jump on.

And there is no hand to grab.

Just as impossible is the notion of the wheel ever stopping.

It cannot.

So, we are separate.

Though I know you are there,

You can only blow me kisses.

You know I am here,

But I can only wave,

And try to feel the memory of your hand in mine.

Journal entry late July 2017:

People talk of grieving or healing, and I believe I have done plenty of both, though I may never be truly done. For how am I to get over losing you?

Your essence, and the invisible touch of your heart to my heart, is as close as my breath. At the same time, the memory of your smell, the sound of your voice, the feel of your hair is harder to recall, as if your physical being continues to get farther and farther away.

I can wrap myself around the idea of grieving – that dull ache, that subtle interruption, that emptiness, and the weariness of continuing without you. Grieving comes. I do not have to look for it or meet it in any particular place. I let myself feel all the shades of it, in hopes that the more I entertain grief, the less often it will come begging at my door. But healing? I'm not sure what healing looks like in this situation.

For me, grief felt like being in the middle of a spherical bubble filled with nothing but a void, keeping me separate from the rest of the world. Like an untouchable, I moved through parties and social settings as if I were invisible, not engaging with strangers. During the first few years, I was focused on the business of relocating and restarting my life, while trying to retain the feeling of Steve's love in the midst of loss.

I really had no interest in finding a new person to fill the hole left by Steve and honestly, I didn't have much to give. My friends asked, "When are you going to start dating again?" I couldn't even entertain the idea. How could I possibly give my attention to someone else, when I wasn't ready to be without Steve?

I wrote to him and asked.

Journal entry August 2017:

My sweet Steve,

After other relationships, healing involved totally letting go, with the objective of completely severing all emotional ties and clearing my heart. After you left, I first tried holding you in my heart, surrounding myself

with things that reminded me of you, trying to keep
you as my one and only true love, hoping to feel your
love and support continuously. That would be enough
for me, but it wasn't possible to feel you fully.

Then, I experimented with thinking I might heal
and move on if I followed the process of healing after
a break-up – remembering the bad times and
disappointments. That idea didn't work at all.

Then I tried putting you in the role of a Spirit
Guide only, in hopes that some other love could come
in without me feeling unfaithful or adulterous. But
somehow, even when I know you are only able to
connect in the non-physical, being with someone else
would still feel like a betrayal.

I don't know how to exclude you, nor do I want
to. How does this work? I wish you could tell me.

As I was writing, a soft voice became present in
the back of my mind. I kept writing, as if taking
dictation: "Just love again."

That's it? No details?

Then came the words, "I will guide you bit by bit.
Don't think about it too much. Just be okay with

whatever you are feeling and trust that I am taking care of you. I will be very present while you are on your own. When you find the right one, I will step aside. It will feel like a natural transition, for my love will continue to come through, but in a joyful, not painful way."

Long pause, while the tears rolled down my cheeks and his soothing words poured down to fill my empty heart.

"You deserve to love and be loved again."

Chapter 20

Trying to Love Again

Spending several years living on my own, without Steve or any other relationship, gave me an opportunity to do what I had not done in previous decades, when my desire for partnership was a driving force.

Since moving to Bozeman, I was able to cultivate a wide circle of women friends and a supportive spiritual community, which filled my need for deep connection. With renewed creative energy, I immersed myself in ceramics classes and eventually built my own studio, filling my kitchen cabinets with hand-made items.

Returning my full attention to my professional career, I picked up where I'd left off with some publishing projects, developed additional techniques and teaching programs, and continued traveling and working in Japan.

Now totally on my own, I took advantage of the opportunity to exercise a new level of independence and self-sufficiency. The house I had purchased needed quite a few cosmetic renovations, so I began doing home improvement projects. Some were simple, like replacing light and bathroom fixtures and building shelves in closets and the garage. Replacing the rotten back deck with a small landing and stairs was more complex, so I teamed up for the project with a neighbor woman who was a professional and I learned how to use power tools!

Being self-reliant gave me a new level of confidence, and I finally felt more settled in my new life. Like water beginning to flow into an empty streambed, the idea of dating started to come to life within me. The notion was a bit daunting, as I wasn't sure of how to go about meeting anyone, nor how it all worked these days. At least I wasn't totally shut off to the concept.

I eased into the local social scene by going out with friends to live music events, one of my favorite activities. There were a number of men who looked to be on their own and in my age bracket, though no telling if they were really single or not.

Once I became open to the idea of meeting someone, there was an internal shift, as if I somehow miraculously transformed from invisible to being noticed.

Having been shut down and hiding away for so long, it was fun to flirt a little. The idea of anything more was intimidating. After any brief encounter, I found myself quickly moving away like a shy schoolgirl. Boy, was I rusty!

In the next phase, I would only put my toe in the water, dating a bit but not letting myself get emotionally involved. Then I decided to totally hold off until I met someone whom I could really connect with, so I wouldn't keep disappointing my 'suitors.'

One night, there was a popular band playing at a local venue, and a female friend and I were planning to go. At the last minute, something came up and she wasn't able to join me. I thought about staying home alone, again, but instead, I decided to be brave and go on my own.

Like a little kid being urged by an invisible friend, I kept hearing Steve's voice in the back of my mind. "You're going to meet someone."

When I first arrived at the show, there were hardly any cars in the parking lot, so I stayed in my car until more people arrived. As I waited, I amused myself by scrolling through photos on my phone and landed on one of the few I kept of Steve. I stared at his smiling face for quite a long time.

From his eyes came... "My Love. You will always be loved." Grateful for his tender encouragement, I left my phone in the car and went in.

Entering the dark room, I was relieved to spot some acquaintances and for the next few songs, I had fun dancing in the group. Beside me was a man who caught my eye and we started talking. This was the first time that I had felt even a little sparkle in my heart since Steve. I was hopeful, excited, and a bit nervous as I let go of my resistance to romance.

As this new man and I began dating, we enjoyed dancing and live music. It was wonderful to again have a companion for meals and social activities. He had many good qualities, like generosity, tenderness, and loyalty, and I could tell he was very fond of me. Yet, I couldn't ignore the niggling concerns that kept popping into my mind.

Were we too different? Had he really gotten over his recent divorce from a long marriage? How should I reconcile my internal conflict of loving this new man, while holding Steve in my heart?

One night, before sleep, my mind was in turmoil. I mulled over all the reasons that I should end the relationship, as if looking for a way to avoid my confusion and conflicted emotions.

Speaking out loud to Steve, I implored, "What am I to do!"

In the morning, as I walked past the kitchen table, I spotted the list of chores that I had made the night before. Only now, there was a rather large gray feather sitting directly atop my *TO DO* list!

Where had it come from?

I don't have any feathers lying about, I live alone, and in the winter, I keep all the doors and windows shut. There were other times when I have found feathers in auspicious places, but always on the ground outside. This was the first time I found one inside! Like *someone* put it RIGHT where I would find it.

With overwhelming emotion, I felt myself bathed in a wave of Steve's ongoing love and support. I sat and stared at the feather as the lump of anxiety in my belly began to melt. I closed my eyes in hopes of receiving a more specific message.

"I'm still with you. Stop being afraid of making mistakes. I won't let anything terrible happen. Being loving brings more love. Just be. Enjoy the moment."

Relieved by the wisdom and tenderness of his words, I adopted a new attitude and kept repeating to myself, "Be okay with whatever happens." I continued the relationship and allowed myself to love more freely. There were even moments when I felt Steve's energy come through at the same time, but not in a disloyal or creepy way. Just more love.

Having a loving partner again was a soothing balm to my wounded heart. Steve had been telling me that he was going to help me find love again, and here it was. I would do my best not to run and hide!

After a few months, I came to the realization that even though there was a strong affection between us, there were also too many unworkable differences. This first real relationship after Steve didn't last, but I know the attempt wasn't a mistake. Rather, more like a reminder of what was possible and an opportunity to taste love again.

A few years later, I became fond of a man with whom I met in a group setting. We enjoyed talking and sharing stories about our spiritual experiences. Though our backgrounds were extremely different, and our ages were too far apart for a lasting relationship, we enjoyed a strong heart and soul connection.

Because of the unchangeable limitations, I had set in my mind that it was probably wisest to keep to a 'friends only' status. Returning to my car after a long evening talking after dinner, I was once again surprised by something I couldn't explain.

Prior to parking and locking my car that evening, I had discarded a half-full plastic water bottle onto the floor of the passenger side. The bottle had baked in my hot car all day and I was sure I wouldn't be drinking from it again.

Now, back from dinner and sitting in the driver seat, I found that same water bottle, *OPEN*, and sitting on the center console, with the cap beside it.

I know myself, and I have never - inadvertently or otherwise – left the lid off a bottle in the car, nor would I set a drink on top of the console when the unused cup holder was right there. In my moment of surprise, I sensed a presence so strongly that I actually turned around to make sure there was no one in the back seat! All clear.

Having gotten somewhat used to these odd physical occurrences, I turned my head upwards to address the culprit! "Okay, Steve. What are you trying to tell me?"

The instant response in my mind, "BE OPEN."

Once again, I was simultaneously astounded and reassured. After so many years, I had assumed that Steve's presence would wane, and now he was showing me that he was still with me. He was still getting my attention, still offering support. I drove home smiling and shaking my head in amusement.

After that night, I allowed myself to become more involved with this kind and interesting man, even though I knew our connection would likely be temporary. Instead of trying to make the relationship something it could not be, which would only result in drama and suffering, we both approached our moments together as mutually healing. I am grateful that when the time came to step back, we could remain as friends.

Though neither one of these relationships was 'the real deal,' I wouldn't interpret Steve's guidance as leading me astray. Rather, I embrace the notion that he is encouraging me to love again. Though my desire for a second soul mate is ever in the back of my mind as a possibility, I'm not chasing the idea.

I am blessed to have had such an authentic and profound love even once in my life. Because of my time with Steve, I know what a truly compatible and loving relationship feels like and I won't settle for less.

Chapter 21

The Impossible IS Possible

There have been so many mysterious occurrences since Steve's death. From that first phone message and roadrunner to the slide show with the moving photo, to the multiple feathers showing up, and numerous physical things being altered or moved, I have been amazed as well as reassured and comforted.

There are no tangible explanations, no proof of the after-death communication I became accustomed to. Perhaps because I needed so badly to not lose Steve completely, or because I was open-minded, I have been able to experience an ongoing inexplicable magic, a touch of the infinite.

Without the physical manifestations, and the many bizarre incidents that were shared and witnessed by others, I might not have kept my antennae alert (as Steve had advised me to do before he died). I might have missed the value of interactions with him in my dreams. I might not have listened to his voice in my mind or followed his guidance for healing. If I hadn't believed that the impossible was possible, I would have missed the magic.

Like Steve used to tell me while watching a movie, "Suspend disbelief!" That was his way of reminding me not to focus too much on needing to *know*, but to simply enjoy.

I had to get out of my rational mind to experience the mystery, to play with unlimited possibilities. Otherwise, it would be tempting to write it all off as coincidence or wishful thinking. Without an expanded perspective, I might have become mired in bitterness and grief. I would have missed the heart healing and blessings coming to me.

My contact with Steve, from the vast unknown, has given me hope for my future, instead of perceiving his death as 'the end.' With this ongoing contact, I've stopped focusing on his illness and my loss, or his and I have avoided getting stuck living only in memories from the past.

Before and after his death, Steve has taught me that once we have touched true love, we can feel it everywhere. I have come to realize that all the love he and I cultivated while together remains in my heart. It's firmly planted there and continues to grow. Even though Steve's physical presence is gone, the love stays. What a gift.

From the other side, as in person, he has taught me that I deserve love and a good life, and to reach farther than the limits of my perception. More than ever before, I pay attention to the subtleties of life and am open to the wondrous potential of tomorrow.

With a full heart and fond memories, I can simply look up into the great beyond and smile. Thank you, Steve. The blessing of you is with me always. Because of you, I am open, but no longer broken.

THE IMPOSSIBLE IS POSSIBLE

Chapter 22

Recommended Methods

This is the 'how to' section of my story, an explanation of some of my methods which may enhance your ability to have your own after-death communication and healing.

Make a plan. If possible, have a conversation with your loved one before they die. Ask, as I did, for an intention to stay connected, and establish a particular way to recognize how they might send you a sign. Maybe a bird, or butterflies, or a favorite song. Perhaps a blinking light in the house or the appearance of a meaningful symbol.

Be open to the mystery. Entertain the idea of possibilities, even if other people might think you unreasonable. Keep your antennae on!

Journal and write letters. Developing a practice of journaling is valuable, as a process of moving through grief, as well as a way to speak to your loved one when they are no longer alive. Trust that they will be able to receive your thoughts in this way. Writing keeps the line of communication open and strong.

Receiving messages in meditation. When you desire a message from your loved one, begin by getting calm first, in a place away from other people or stimuli, even if you only have a short moment. Focus your attention on the love you shared, remembering the warm feeling. Ask a simple question of the person and be open to trusting the first response that pops into your mind. It may take several attempts to move past the expectations of your own thoughts, but keep trying.

Visits in the dream world. Your loved one may show up in your dreams, especially in the first days or weeks after their passing. To best remember your dreams, keep your eyes closed upon waking and allow any dreams to replay in your mind's eye. If you jump right into your day's activities, dreams evaporate. To increase the likelihood of a dream appearance, before you go to sleep at night, ask your loved one to show up in your dream. Ask them to bring you a message, or simply ask for comfort and reassurance.

Reconnect your heart cord. Close your eyes and bring your attention to your heart. Only witnessing, not suffering, become aware of a sensation, perhaps an ache or tension. Perhaps you sense the pain of a gaping hole. There is an invisible cord that once connected the two of you, heart to heart. The cord is still attached to you, but the other end is loose. With the power of your imagination, redirect the cord into the Spirit realm. Visualize your loved one grabbing the loose end and restoring a link, through them, to a universal source of love. Feel your heart being filled and healed.

Seeking Professional Advice. You may find value in reaching out to those skilled in connecting with the other side, as I did. If so, please use your own wise discernment in knowing who to trust and whether their messages have truth and value for you, or not.

Learn to trust your intuition. Only you know what you are comfortable with and what you need in any situation. The trick is to believe your intuition, rather than discounting it, and to act on what is best for you. There may be additional strategies to help with loss that come through your own higher wisdom, or as direct instruction from your loved one. Experiment, practice, and hold onto what works.

Epilogue

When I mentioned to friends that I was writing this story, several of them told of their own ongoing appearances of Steve. One friend reported, "In times of confusion or self-doubt, I see Steve's face, complete with those twinkling blue eyes and even all his wrinkles. He doesn't say anything, but I feel his love and encouragement." Others reported that they sometimes see Steve in their peripheral vision, which at first catches them off guard, but then is reassuring.

Though I miss Steve's physical presence, I can still feel his energy and love whenever I want to. My focus on him seems to call him in. I continue to have dreams of sharing and comfort with Steve simply lying beside me, letting me know I am not alone. And since beginning to write this book, his presence has become stronger. I can easily picture him smiling at me as I write. In fact, I feel a bit prodded by him to finish!

I recall one of Steve's earliest messages. "Remember our story. Tell it to others." Now I understand the importance, not only for those who are curious about what's on the other side, but in the value of him and I staying connected, for love's sake.

Writing our story has also provided an opportunity for me to process my trauma with less emotional intensity, bringing greater resolution. I am now more fully accepting of Steve's passing, as I embrace meaningful realizations that may not have come to me without the writing.

I also have a more thorough understanding of our soul agreement. The most evident human part of our soul agreement while Steve was alive was to support each other in achieving professional goals, to help each other heal from difficult childhood experiences, and to demonstrate our version of a beautiful relationship.

Reflecting on the past life journey exploration he and I did when we first met, I now better understand the clues in those experiences as an indication of what we were to do for each other, on a soul level. Steve helped me once again become the Priestess in the Temple, and I helped the Apache return to his desert homeland.

Even after Steve's death, our soul agreement continues to evolve. From the other side, he has provided wisdom about what lies beyond death, and shown me ways of healing that I wouldn't have discovered on my own.

I am pleased to be sharing the messages and specific techniques that were shown to me and which helped me to process my grief. I find grace in knowing that all of this – the love, the loss, the healing, and now the sharing – is part of my soul purpose.

While writing this story, I was inspired to open a box of photo prints and love letters from when Steve and I were first falling in love and living apart. This box had not been opened since packing to move to Marfa. Among the photos which show us both shining with delight, I rediscovered a beautiful art print that he had made and mailed to me.

Beneath the small image were the words "I Love You" written in pencil. I remembered this one, but there was something that wasn't there before.

A very small and soft feather is now stuck firmly to the paper. I smile. He is still at it!

EPILOGUE

Acknowledgments

Among the many people who helped me along the journey of this story, I would like to specifically thank Joe and Lauri McCarthy (brother and sister of my heart), Elizabeth Blackman (*Healing Touch*), Cherry Divine (Intuitive Counselor), Staci French (Psychic and Medium), and Jason Snell (friend and Attorney extraordinaire).

In the writing and editing of this book, I am grateful to Marc Hannon, Nancy Peters, and Sandy Reinschmidt for their invaluable feedback and finetuning.

And of course, Steve Holzer, for continuing to bring clarity and added energy from the other side, assisting me as I share our story.

About the Author

Daeryl Holzer is an internationally recognized Clairvoyant and Spiritual Teacher. For over 25 years, she has been guiding others to clear limiting beliefs and overcome difficult situations. Her focus is seeing life from the soul perspective and empowering people with compassion and practical life wisdom.

Author of *Opening A Window To The Soul: A Guide to Living Beyond the Human Drama*, *The Spirit Game*, and *Permissions: 100 Days of Encouragement*, Daeryl has also developed several teaching programs; *SoulShift Healing Process*™, Past Life Healing, and Clairvoyant Development, all of which include her specialized techniques and innovative guided journeys.

Now living in Bozeman, Montana, Daeryl enjoys kayaking, swimming, skiing, camping, ceramics, and dancing. She is available for speaking, teaching, private sessions, and mentoring. She can be reached via www.daerylholzer.com.